China's Military Reforms

About the Book and Editors

China's reform policies during the past decade have resulted in the reorganization of economic and political structures and have led to a dramatic reorientation of the nation's foreign policy. These reforms have especially influenced China's military establishment, which is now in a period of major transition. What new paradigm is replacing the old Maoist model of People's War, however, is not clear. This book examines what China's military modernization means for the global and regional balance of power and for China's internal political-economic system. Specific chapters focus on changes in Chinese strategy and doctrine, developments in defense industries and military procurements, China's acquisition of foreign technology, its military education system, and its nuclear weapons program.

Colonel Charles D. Lovejoy, Jr., is professor of military science and commander of the Army ROTC detachment at Princeton University. *Commander Bruce W. Watson* is director of publications at the Defense Intelligence College. He is the editor of numerous military studies, including *The Soviet Navy* (Westview, 1986).

China's Military Reforms

International and
Domestic Implications

edited by Charles D. Lovejoy, Jr.,
and Bruce W. Watson

Westview Press / Boulder and London

Westview Special Studies in Military Affairs

The views expressed in this book are solely those of the authors and do not represent the positions or policies of any agency or department of the United States Government. The following chapters were derived from unclassified publications and sources and are intended to neither confirm nor deny, officially or unofficially, the views of the United States Government.

This Westview softcover edition was manufactured on our own premises using equipment and methods that allow us to keep even specialized books in stock. It is printed on acid-free paper and bound in softcovers that carry the highest rating of the National Association of State Textbook Administrators, in consultation with the Association of American Publishers and the Book Manufacturers' Institute.

All rights reserved. No part of this publication may be reproduced or transmitted in any form or by any means, electronic or mechanical, including photocopy, recording, or any information storage and retrieval system without permission in writing from the publisher.

Copyright © 1986 by Westview Press, Inc.

Published in 1986 in the United States of America by Westview Press, Inc.; Frederick A. Praeger, Publisher; 5500 Central Avenue, Boulder, Colorado 80301

Library of Congress Cataloging in Publication Data
China's military reforms.
  (Westview special studies in military affairs)
  Includes index.
  1. China--Armed Forces. 2. China--Politics and government--1976-
3. China--Foreign relations--1976-   . I. Lovejoy, Charles D. II. Watson, Bruce W. III. Series.
UA835.C4468 1986   355'.00951   86-7757
ISBN 0-8133-7216-X (alk. paper)

Composition for this book was provided by the editors.
This book was produced without formal editing by the publisher.

Printed and bound in the United States of America

∞ The paper used in this publication meets the minimum requirements of the American National Standard for Permanence of Paper for Printed Library Materials Z39.48-1984.

6 5 4 3 2 1

To Doug and Marian Lovejoy

Contents

PREFACE, CHINA AND ITS MILITARY MODERNIZATION: THE PROBLEM OF PERSPECTIVES, ... xi

ACKNOWLEDGMENTS xix

1. PEOPLE'S WAR REVISED: MILITARY DOCTRINE, STRATEGY, AND OPERATIONS, Paul H. B. Godwin 1

2. THE INTERPLAY OF SCIENCE AND TECHNOLOGY IN CHINESE MILITARY MODERNIZATION, William T. Tow 15

3. IMPLICATIONS OF THE POST-MAO REFORMS ON THE CHINESE DEFENSE INDUSTRIES, Richard J. Latham 35

4. FOREIGN TECHNOLOGY AND CHINESE MODERNIZATION, Wendy Frieman . 51

5. CHINESE WEAPONS DEVELOPMENT: PROCESS, PROGRESS, PROGRAM? John Frankenstein 69

6. THE REFORM OF MILITARY EDUCATION IN CHINA: AN OVERVIEW, William R. Heaton and Charles D. Lovejoy, Jr. 91

7. DEVELOPMENTS IN CHINA'S NUCLEAR WEAPONS AND ATTITUDES TOWARD ARMS CONTROL, Robert G. Sutter 101

8. SUMMARY: CHINA'S MILITARY MODERNIZATION: A SYSTEMIC ANALYSIS, Robert E. Johnson, Jr. 111

ABOUT THE EDITORS AND CONTRIBUTORS 129

INDEX 133

Preface
China and Its Military Modernization: The Problem of Perspectives

"Empires wax and wane." So opens China's epic novel of power politics and military strategy, The Romance of the Three Kingdoms. After a century and a half of turmoil and revolution, China's position seems to be "waxing" and it is doing so in a world of rapidly shifting power balances. Structures of international systems, like empires, also rise and fall. Pax Britannica gave way to Pax Americana. Now the apparent relative decline of the postwar international structure underwritten by U.S. political, economic, and military power is a central strategic issue. The apparent relative decline in U.S. power and influence in the last decade has been a major factor in the renewal of Chinese influence in global affairs.

The prominent role of the Chinese People's Liberation Army (PLA) in the celebration of the thirty-fifth anniversary of the People's Republic of China (PRC) underscores the importance of this book's subject, the systemic implications of China's military modernization. Since October 1, 1949, China's role in the global balance has evolved through several stages: from a close partnership with the Soviet Union during the tight bipolar structure of the cold war, through a period of hostile isolationism in the loose bipolar structure of the 1960's, to a strategic leaning toward the United States as a counterweight to the Soviet Union in the 1980s. Indeed, as in The Romance of the Three Kingdoms, China has been at the center of a classic three cornered maneuvering for the balance of power. Throughout these somewhat turbulent stages of strategic development, China's goal has remained essentially the same--development of a modern socialist economy under communist party leadership within a favorable international environment. Policies of close identification with the Soviet Union and subsequent isolationism failed to achieve this objective. Now China has turned to the West with significant implications for the operation and structure of the international system.

The implications of China's military modernization and new position of relative power go beyond the simple, though hard, assessments of the rise and fall of empires, global systems, and their members. The title of this book implies a relationship between China's efforts to improve its military capabilities and its relationships with the outside world. National power is the sum of the components of power and the application of those components in the development of unique national security strategies.

With regard to the components of national power--general economic development, defense industry, military systems and organizations, morale, and doctrine--China is undergoing significant change. How China's military modernization relates to the question of change in the international structure, therefore, is the overall theme of the chapters of this work.

The scope of the term "systems," as used in this book, however, is somewhat specific. While in the broadest sense, "system" encompasses international relations themes such as balance of power and systemic structure (bipolar, multi-polar, etc.), here it will be used in a more narrow sense in order to focus on specific changes in China's defense industries, military organizations and doctrines, and the mechanics of how China conducts military-related business with the outside world. The most difficult task in contemporary strategic analysis is to integrate broad and narrow gauged analyses. This book does not attempt to integrate these two levels of analysis as much as it summarizes current thought in specific areas of this question and lays the groundwork for further research.

Some discussion of the theoretical issues, however, is necessary. A more literal translation of the opening lines of the Romance may more accurately reflect the systemic nature of the issue. "In the great affairs under heaven; what is in chaos must become harmonious; what is harmonious must become chaotic" (Tian xia da shi: fen jiu bi he; he jiu bi fen). China's new strategic position within the international system will be the result of the coming together of a myriad of smaller systems of domestic and foreign policy decisionmaking, all of which have been greatly influenced by the post-Mao policies of reform set in motion by the 3rd Plenum of the 11th Central Committee in August 1978.

The most important objective of these reforms is to overcome the disastrous effects of radical Maoist policies on China's political and economic structures. Deng Xiaoping's deft handling of PLA leadership, where support for Maoist principles and programs has remained strongest, has demonstrated his ability to create a consensus on the importance of military modernization. With regard to actual systemic improvements in the Chinese defense establishment, however, there remain two different obstacles, the lingering influence of Soviet organizational models and weapons technology, and traditional Chinese bureaucratic tendency to operate vertically with little horizontal consideration between units. China appears to be suspended between past Soviet technological and organizational influences, which it rejected, and future U.S. influence, which it fears.

IMPORTANCE OF THEORY: STRATEGIC TRADE-OFFS

Foreign policy analysis often fluctuates between two general schools of thought. Both acknowledge the importance of national security and promotion of national interests. However, they differ in their approaches to achieving these objectives. The first school emphasizes the importance of military capability as the key to security, while the second emphasizes the importance of alternative forms of power, such as economic, diplomatic, and cultural. For the first school, often espoused by balance of power proponents, the systemic importance of the U.S. entre to China is rationalized in terms of the "strategic balance" between the United States and the Soviet Union. Alternatively, the second school, loosely composed of interdependency and integration theorists, emphasizes the importance of interactions in the international system, and points to the strategic importance of integrating China into the larger world community through trade and social/cultural interaction.

Realist theories of international relations focus squarely on national military capabilities as the source of nation-centered rational behavior. Some theorists stress survival, while others, like Morgenthau, have elaborated on the importance of understanding power as an end in itself. While the utility of force in the nuclear age, specifically the appropriate calculation and use of deterrent force, has been debated in international relations circles, few analysts argue against the ultimate importance of military capabilities in underwriting national self-interests.

While China is no exception to this proposition, it has been a unique international case. Except in the most simplistic terms, China is very difficult to fit into most western analytical models of the balance of power or systemic behavior because of its unique historical experience, self-contained culture, and its thirty year, ambiguous implementation of communist ideology. China is even more difficult to evaluate in terms of academic disciplines related to modernization, that is, those fields which emphasize development, interdependence, or integration.

Foreign analysts bemoan the difficulty of fitting Chinese data into general academic models or applying these models when assessing the Chinese experience. This difficulty is as true for military studies as it is for the other sectors of Chinese life. But it also points to the unique nature of the systemic implications of Chinese military modernization. From a balance of power perspective, developing modern military capabilities not only will give China the power to play a more active role in the international arena, but also will change China's interests significantly. This perspective implies an increased threat to U.S. security and national interests, since a militarily strong China, regardless of its ideological persuasion, would be a matter of serious concern to the United States and Japan, and our Asian allies. More importantly, given the continued leadership of the Chinese Communist Party, the unspoken U.S. concern inevitably is that China, with a modern military establishment, would be able to support effectively an expansion of its communist ideology.

From an interdependence viewpoint, however, China's military modernization also offers a political perspective of a different sort. The influx of modern weapons technology and its attendant baggage of support systems potentially acts as a penetrating solvent on society through direct influence on the structure and operation of the industrial process, and indirectly, through influence on the individual soldiers who operate the equipment and train in its new deployment methods. Mao and the leaders of the Cultural Revolution recognized this social threat and reacted strongly against PLA factions which stressed the importance of new weapons technology in the 1960s. The leading role of the military in the modernization process is well demonstrated and argued in Western literature. In the case of China, military modernization, along with attendant economic, political, and social reform designed to create a modern socialist society, opens the door once again to increased integration and compatibility with the West. The unspoken U.S. hope in this regard is that modernization will erode the impact of militant Marxism-Leninism, if not undermine the system entirely.

These two theoretical approaches to analyzing China's role within the international structure (power and balance vs. interdependence) further frame the strategic issue for U.S. policy. Recently, this policy has supported active military cooperation. Underlying this policy are the remaining doubts expressed in the debate between those who view a strong China as a potential friend or ally and those who view China as a potential foe. The argument is further refined by considerations such as changing Chinese interests based on its expanded economic power and international position. Even a friendly China, when it becomes a truly global actor, will have interests that require big power attention. Finally, there is the argument based almost purely on theory that, whether friend or foe, a strong China will side with neither the United States nor the Soviet Union, but will, through an independent position supported by a modern military establishment, preserve the international balance of power.

Conversely, in the interdependence school, there is relatively less debate over the benefit of relations with China, which, in the main, is seen as the peaceful integration of China into the world market system through economic interaction. Certainly the economic reforms and opening to the West under Deng's reform program seem to support the case for the positive influence of the integration theory. The reforms may not lead ultimately to the Western ideal of a non-communist liberal democracy in an economically strong China. Nonetheless, the evolving pattern of regional economic action and power balances which is now evident probably more closely resembles the objectives of the classic U.S. Open Door policy toward China than at any other time in the history of Sino-American relations.

Power analysts, who are concerned with assessing the balance of international power in order to insure survival, support the positive systems implications of China's role in balancing power between the United States and the Soviet Union. Integrationists, whose intent is to look beyond national power considerations for the sake of global stability, support the systems implications of China's openness to world market influences.

These two dissimilar, but complementary, approaches to analyzing systemic influences point to the two different levels of analysis in assessing the impact of China's military modernization. More importantly, they hint of a third level of analysis, which ultimately may prove to be the most important consideration in assessing systemic change in China. The first level is an understanding of the macro issue of how China will influence regional and global power balances. What military and diplomatic measures will China's neighbors take to offset or accomodate China's new strength resulting from this modernization? Will they strengthen themselves independently, seek multilateral alliances with the United States or the Soviet Union, or seek to accomodate China under terms of traditional Chinese hegemony? Globally, will a potential U.S.-Japanese-Chinese consortium, aimed however indirectly at the Soviet Union, lead to Soviet accomodations with Western Europe which eventually would result in a dramatic confrontation between Pacific powers, including the United States, and a Soviet-European alliance? Such is the stuff of systems and balance of power theories.

On the micro level there are questions of more direct relevance to the various sub-systems within the national units. These are the stuff of interdependence theories. How will China's economic reforms affect patterns of political decisionmaking in social relationships? How will Chinese efforts to learn about and participate in such undertakings as nuclear power agreements, world trade protocols, and arms control negotiations, affect both their world view and their view of themselves? The complex web of interrelationships woven about technical issues of arms sales and technology transfers brings to China the same array of internal systemic issues that Western industrialized nations face with the increased computerization of their economies and societies.

The last question leads to the third level of analysis and resurrects an old issue which has existed since the confrontation between rising Western imperialism and the declining Ching empire at the end of the 19th Century. This problem is China's ability to absorb Western scientific thought without losing its distinct national character. This issue often has been noted in comparisons between China and Japan, and it is argued that since Japan absorbed Western technology and developed a modern industrial state without loss of national identity, China should be able to do so as well. Here a wide variety of answers generally fall into two categories: either that the strength of China's Confucian tradition prevented an open official experimentation like Japan's under the Meiji; or the impact of Maoist ideology moved China too quickly along Marxist-Leninist lines of socialist revolution. After the failures of the Ching Reform movement, the Nationalist Revolution, the alliance with the Soviet Union, and the Cultural Revolution, China is still searching for its own road to modernization. The new era of Deng pragmatism can thus be viewed as another attempt by the Chinese leadership to resolve this century-old dilemma.

THE ROLE OF THE MILITARY

The PLA plays a central role in China's attempt to resolve this dilemma. On the micro level, military modernization means assessing the impact of technical changes, and absorbing modern technology, new training methods, and new approaches to military doctrine and strategy. On the macro level, military modernization means giving China the capability to act more assertively and positively in influencing regional and global affairs. The link between these two levels is the issue of strategy, since a militarily weak China has had to develop an appropriate military strategy. This strategy has been People's War, which deters on the basis of China's one strategic strength but current economic weakness, its population. A militarily strong China can develop a military strategy to support a more open, more assertive role in regional and global affairs. However, by incorporating Western technology and systems, China will also develop close economic ties with the West with attendant economic and social compatibilities. Conversely, if China fails to achieve military modernization, then it will be because of its incompatibility with modern technology and its failure to adapt to the demands of mechanical and technical discipline and well grounded, creative applications of technology. To the extent that this failure will be due to either the traditional features of Chinese culture or to the ideological characteristics of the communist regime, it will be the result of the interplay of domestic and international politics. Failure to meet a similar challenge at the turn of the century led to the collapse of an empire and continued foreign intervention and dominance for another fifty years. The Chinese leadership is too sensitive to this lesson not recognize the potential of its happening again.

GENERAL THEMES OF THE SYSTEMIC IMPLICATIONS

There are several themes, therefore, that provide a common thread through the chapters in this book: Chinese dissatisfaction with the old way of doing things, investigating new approaches, experimenting with changes within specific fields or systems, and concern over the impact of potential changes on the system of political control.

The idea for this book grew out of two panel discussions held during a Defense Intelligence College-sponsored panel at the International Studies Association Section on Military Studies (SOMS) at the U.S. Air Force Academy in October 1984. Among American specialists, it has been apparent for some time, that the nature of China's military system would change as the country itself changes. While much attention has been paid to the implications of changing Chinese geopolitical and military strategy, especially within the context of the U.S.-Chinese "strategic relationship," to date there has been little assessment of how the various reforms are affecting China's military establishment. It is the purpose of this book to contribute to this task.

The link between analyzing systemic issues of a strategic nature--the balance of power and the system of international relations--and analyzing the systemic impact of domestic programs and policies is strategy itself.

Paul Godwin's chapter outlines the objectives of Chinese military strategy and examines the dilemmas in making the transition from People's War to People's War Under Modern Conditions. Development of a modern economy creates new strategic demands on the PLA, namely the need for a forward defense of territory and an adequate deterrence strategy in order to preserve new industrial centers. Chinese evaluation of strategic objectives in providing this new type of defense necessarily includes evaluation of both tactical and strategic nuclear options. More importantly, new theater weapons such as the Soviet SS-20 or the U.S. Pershing missile are now included in power balance calculations that influence Chinese deliberations on force development and doctrinal changes. For the Chinese in recent years, a hard look at the elements and issues of nuclear strategy and arms control has forced a reevaluation of traditional attitudes toward those two critical components of the international balance of power. Robert Sutter's chapter on this subject traces recent shifts in Chinese attitudes toward the critical issues and their apparent openness to participate in international deliberations on arms control.

The new, rapid growth of China's economy points initially to the probable success of Deng's modernization programs. However, economic success does not automatically translate into an increased defense capability. The reorganization of inefficient organs of defense decisionmaking has accompanied a general reorganization of China's political and economic infrastructure. William Tow investigates this reorganization and speculates on its implications for China's participation in the world market. Wendy Frieman then examines the Chinese approach to the study and incorporation of foreign technology and weapon systems into China's research, development, and production cycles. Her chapter, along with John Frankenstein's chapter on Chinese scientific and technical development patterns, provide a unique picture of how domestic and foreign elements collaborate, or do not collaborate, in contributing to China's development of its military industries. Finally, Richard Latham's chapter provides a needed review of the weapons production cycle, and of how scientific and technological inputs from both domestic and foreign sources, find their way through the Chinese military system to the field.

Underwriting the changes in strategic doctrine and development in defense production is often referred to as the software side of the military capabilities equation. Successful strategic deployments and technical improvements rely ultimately on the soldier's abilities to meet the challenge of using modern equipment on the battlefield, commanders and their staffs to integrate new technical capabilities into an effective doctrine, and workers and technicians to produce reliable equipment in the factory and laboratory. The proper mix of well trained and motivated soldiers has been a critical modern issue for China, as evidenced in the traditional period by the Chinese defeat at the hands of modern Japanese forces in 1895 and 1905, in the revolutionary period by the development of the Whampoa Military Academy in 1921 to provide modern training and political leadership, and in the Maoist period by the confrontation between technicians and politicians over the Lo Juiching incident prior to the Cultural Revolution.

The present Chinese military leadership has ascribed a position of strategic importance to military education. Major reforms have been underway within the PLA, the most important of which have been related to education and training. William Heaton's chapter summarizes these reforms and evaluates the potential directions and problems. A more professional, educationally oriented officer corps, drawn heavily from urban areas, will be different from the traditional, rurally-oriented Maoist era PLA. The transition period will not be easy as the military will be forced to compete with civilian industries for well-educated, technically competent personnel.

In his concluding chapter, Robert Johnson sums up the findings and evaluations put forward in the previous chapters and contributes his own view on the strategic implications of this development.

In summary, this book contributes to a new genre of literature on the PLA and the Chinese miltary. The golden age, so to speak, of Chinese military assessments covered the period of the late 1920s through the early 1970s. The basic Maoist model of a politically oriented, guerilla inspired PLA appears to be passing from the scene with the Maoist system itself. The early works, (by Fred Riggs, Samuel Griffith, Ellis Joffe, John Gittings, Angus Fraser, and especially William Whitson) contributed significantly both to our understanding of the nature of the PLA and to the evolution of the U.S. strategies that contained China and eventually led it to the current path of reform, with all its implications for change in the PLA. The PLA will build on its history as it adapts and reforms; future analysis will build on this history. Both, however, require an understanding of the systemic nature of modern defense problems and the international environment in which they will operate. In short, the "waxing" of the new Chinese "empire" will build on its past as China moves toward reform and attempts to harmonize the elements of its defense system into a modern, effective military establishment. If this volume contributes to an understanding of this process and its implications, then the editors and contributors will have achieved their goal.

Charles D. Lovejoy, Jr.

Acknowledgments

We wish to thank all of the contributors for participating in this study.

We are also indebted to Fred Praeger, Barbara Ellington, and the staff of Westview Press for their advice, assistance, and encouragement.

This study would not have been possible without the encouragement and counsel of many members of the faculty of the Defense Intelligence College. Of these, special mention must be made of Colonel John D. Macartney, U.S. Air Force, the Commandant of the Defense Intelligence College, Dr. Robert L. De Gross, the College's Provost, and its Director of Research, Colonel Douglas A. Ruane, U.S. Army, without whose encouragement and guidance this study would not have been completed.

Without the competent and patient support of the individuals who typed all of the drafts and final versions of the chapters of the book, this work would never have been possible. We are thus indebted to Gloria D. Porche, Norma J. Dorey, and Jacquline D. Cooper.

Finally, we are indebted to Sue Watson and Bruce W. Watson, Jr., who proofread and reviewed the manuscripts, to Jennifer Watson, who assisted in the book's production, and to Susan M. O. Watson, who assisted in the artwork.

Charles D. Lovejoy, Jr.
Bruce W. Watson

1

People's War Revised: Military Doctrine, Strategy, and Operations[1]

Paul H. B. Godwin

INTRODUCTION

The Chinese People's Liberation Army (PLA) is now in the eighth year of a wide-ranging defense modernization program, which is intended for far more than simply updating weapons and equipment. Rather, it seeks to: rebuild the defense industrial base; drastically improve the capabilities of the defense research, development, testing and evaluation (RDT&E) infrastructure; raise the professional qualities of the officer corps; and revise the basic military doctrine, strategy, and military operations by which the PLA plans and conducts war. This chapter will assess the changes occurring in Chinese concepts of military doctrine, strategy, and operations in order to provide a better understanding of the military objectives of the modernization program.

For some years, the Chinese have described the ongoing changes in doctrine and strategy as "People's War under Modern Conditions." Too often, however, the use of this term tends to obfuscate rather than clarify the changes underway. "People's War," as it is commonly understood in the West, raises images of a relentless and protracted war of attrition in which the enemy is destroyed piecemeal--drowned in the sea of a hostile population. It is a concept of "total" war in which the entire society engages the enemy. Yet, in the late 1960s, China began deploying its first nuclear-armed ballistic missiles while the defense industries were producing Chinese versions of an entire range of Soviet-designed conventional arms. Before the current defense modernization program was launched, China had fielded thousands of fixed-wing combat aircraft, tanks, armored personnel carriers, and artillery pieces, and was proceeding toward deploying intercontinental ballistic missiles (ICBMs) and a nuclear-powered ballistic missile submarine (SSBN). Thus before the present program began, the PLA's force structure--the size and composition of the armed forces that form the PLA--did not reflect a doctrine based upon the concepts usually associated with "People's War."

Indeed, what this force structure reflected was an objective sought in China's first period of intense defense modernization when, with the assistance of the USSR, the Chinese military hierarchy sought to build a modern army that would field weapons ranging from tanks and advanced combat aircraft to ballistic missiles. The Sino-Soviet dispute brought an end to Soviet assistance programs in 1959-1960, and internal crises over the next fifteen years drastically reduced China's ability to continue a broad defense modernization program. Many areas of weapons and equipment development stagnated at the level of technology supplied by the USSR in the 1950s, and only the nuclear weapons and the associated space programs continued to make significant progress, albeit erratically.

Today, the continuing development and deployment of increasingly sophisticated nuclear weapons and reconnaissance satellites demonstrates China's commitment to military programs usually associated only with major military powers. Perhaps more important in determining China's long-range modernization goals are the changes occurring in its concepts of military doctrine and strategy. This is not to argue that military technology is unimportant, but to state that by reviewing emerging concepts of doctrine and strategy we can determine, even if only with limited precision, how the military leadership plans to link technology with war. Obviously, the Chinese leadership wishes to achieve a military capability that will allow it to more effectively defend China and Chinese interests. However, by reviewing the concepts of doctrine and strategy that have emerged as the defense modernization program has developed since the late 1970s, we can determine how the military hierarchy wishes to achieve this objective and develop a clearer image of what future military capabilities the Chinese armed forces are being designed to achieve.

Before analyzing Chinese doctrine and strategy it is noteworthy that the principal objective of China's national security policy is to deter war, and that within this policy, political strategy plays the preeminent role. It is also important to ascertain the Chinese military hierarchy's views on the relationship between politics and military capabilities in establishing such a base for deterrence. The defense minister commented in 1983 that:

> To counter the superpowers' hegemonism, defend our country's peaceful construction and safeguard world peace, in addition to carrying out necessary political and diplomatic struggles we must also build a powerful defense behind us. The stronger our national defense, the bigger the guarantee for our peaceful construction and the possibility of suspending and preventing war.[2]

THE PROBLEM OF DOCTRINE

There is considerable disagreement over the definition of "doctrine" and it is important not to impute Western meanings into the Chinese use of the concept. Doctrine can, however, be defined as an authoritative statement of the principles of war to be used as a guide in the development of strategy. It is "authoritative" to the extent that these principles are officially sanctioned by those responsible for determining what doctrine shall be. According to Georges Tan Eng Bok, contemporary Chinese strategic thought is divided into three levels: military doctrine (junshi xueshuo); military science (junshi kexue); and military art (junshi xueshu). Military doctrine is formed at the highest political and military levels and reflects the Chinese Communist Party's (CCP's) military line (junshi luxian). Military doctrine provides the guidance for military science, which is concerned with the general problems involved in conducting war. Within military science, the most important branch of study is military art, which is primarily concerned with problems of strategy (zhanlue), operations (zhanyi), and tactics (zhanshu).[3]

Within this structure, People's War under Modern Conditions has assumed the status of doctrine by providing the principles guiding the development of Chinese military strategy in balance with the technological modernization of the PLA's armament and equipment. Since the late 1970s, much of the public debate over strategy has concentrated on the need to modify Mao Zedong's principles of People's War to fit the problems of contemporary warfare. Chinese analyses of such warfare have focused on the implications of modern technology for military strategy and operations, especially in a "future war against aggression"--the Chinese euphemism for a war with the Soviet Union. Thus military art (junshi xueshu) has become the primary focus of public analyses in much the same manner that it has in the USSR.[4]

The dilemma faced by Chinese strategists is that even though People's War under Modern Conditions has the status of doctrine there is no systematic explication of what this doctrine contains, to the extent that there are no references in Chinese analyses of strategy to a series of documents in which the principles are outlined. In essence this means that the principles of People's War developed by Mao Zedong in the 1930s remain the source of current doctrine as that doctrine is modified by the demands of modern warfare. The complexity of this problem can be seen in Yang Shangkun's essay on the role of the Mao Zedong's military thought in understanding modern warfare. In a manner that has become common since the late 1970s, Mao Zedong's military thought is defined as "the scientific principle that has been tested through practice." This same body of thought, however, "is by no means the end of truth. On the contrary, it has opened up a correct and wide path for us to understand the new problems in military spheres."[5] The emphasis is on practice; on using principles developed through past experience to understand current and future problems. This stress has meant that past doctrinal principles, such as "active defense" (jiji fangyu), are interpreted to fit current situations, and it is such attempts to transform past doctrine to fit current problems that have led to the emphasis on military art, especially strategy and operations, over military doctrine. What appears to be occurring is that, since doctrine developed in the 1930s can be used only loosely as a guide to contemporary problems, military doctrine is emerging as a by-product of current strategy and operations problem-solving.

STRATEGY AND OPERATIONS

As the Chinese develop a strategy that will successfully defend China against a Soviet attack, there are major limitations on what they can expect to achieve over the next decade. They face a superpower along a border extending some 6,500 miles when one includes the Mongolian People's Republic. The area to be defended is large, and the transportation system provides only a limited capability to move heavily equipped forces from one part of China to another. The armed forces field weapons and equipment that, although they are believed to be rugged and serviceable in battle, generally are effective only in daylight when the visibility is good. The logistical support system is weak and would be highly stressed to support an intensive war of the kind Soviet forces are trained and equipped to fight. If the war should go above the conventional level, the Chinese face the dual problem of inferiority in both strategic and battlefield/theater nuclear weapons.

These problems are severe and are not easily resolved. The length of the border, the area to be defended, and low strategic mobility represent continuing problems. Technological improvements are being made in weapons and equipment, but it will be some years before all-weather "over the horizon" capabilities are common to Chinese armaments. The solution that the Chinese have selected is to concentrate their defenses in areas of greatest economic and political value and to leave much of the border only thinly defended. Manchuria and north central China are the areas covered by the Shenyang, Beijing, and Lanzhou military regions. Xinjiang is only lightly defended.[6] The assumption appears to be that a major conventional assault by the USSR will be directed at those areas of greatest economic and political value to China that are within the reach of Soviet forces.

Even though the technological limitations of Chinese armaments will be overcome only slowly, there is strength as well as weakness in low technology systems. To the extent that the Chinese armed forces are not dependent on technological sophistication for communications and target acquisition, they may not be so susceptible to Soviet electronic warfare. The problem arises when an adversary uses advanced military technologies that can disrupt communications systems and destroy low visibility targets, and when the defender has no, or only a limited capability to neutralize the enemy's systems. The extensive debate over simple <u>versus</u> sophisticated systems demonstrates the lack of agreement on this issue. Thus, when reviewing Chinese combat capabilities, it is necessary to indicate the types of restraints the Chinese face as they plan future strategy and military operations. It is an issue the Chinese themselves raise with great frequency.

Even with these limitations, there has been a major change in the strategy the Chinese plan to use in a "future war against aggression." Rather than seeking to defend against a major attack by fighting a classical People's War in which "fortress" China is used to absorb Soviet forces, Chinese strategists now seek to defeat the attacking forces much closer to the border. The weakness identified in the traditional People's War strategy is that the price of "victory" would include all that China had built since 1949.[7] Since 1981, the focus of China's revised strategic concepts has been to defeat the USSR at less cost than that which would be imposed in a People's War.

This view was expressed by Zhang Aiping, China's defense minister when he stated in 1983:

> The principle of war is to achieve the greatest victory at the smallest expense. To achieve this we should depend not only on political factors but also on the correct strategy and tactics of the war's commander, the sophisticated nature of our military equipment, the quality of our personnel who use the equipment, etcetera.[8]

Such a view of war is obviously not unique to the Chinese and brings into focus the link between strategy, military operations, and technology which is common to all military strategy. China is clearly aware of its technological weaknesses, and the 1979 incursion into Vietnam demonstrated to the military leadership the PLA's weaknesses in conducting military operations.[9] Since 1979 there has been a systematic attempt to establish an effective integration of strategy and military operations that both recognizes the technological limitations of the armed forces and makes the most effective use of the forces China can put into the field.

The objective of the strategic revisions that have occurred since the Vietnam incursion is to disrupt and defeat a Soviet invasion of China before it can make a deep penetration. In particular, the Chinese have decided to defend their cities rather than surrender them to the invading forces in order to maintain the freedom to maneuver. This is in sharp contrast to the strategy followed by Mao Zedong's forces in the 1930s and 1940s, when towns could be, and were, vacated in order to maintain the fluidity of the war that is at the core of Mao's principles for the defense of China. Defending cities is now deemed necessary because of their importance as industrial and politcal centers and by the need for an industrial base to support the logistical requirements of the Chinese armed forces.[10] These factors alone have required a significant revision in Mao's doctrinal and strategic concepts.

By seeking to preserve the cities and prevent a deep penetration by Soviet forces, Chinese strategic formulators have had to face the problem of devising military operations that will be successful in the early stages of a war. In fact, this issue has created what may be a very sharp debate among Chinese strategists. Zong He, a research associate at the PLA-run Beijing Institute for Strategic Studies (BISS), has presented the argument that contemporary military technology has made the opening stages of a war far more important than they were in World Wars I and II, and that the initial battles will have a more important role in influencing the course of a war. The reason for this is that the strategic rear areas are no longer safe from attack, therefore it is no longer plausible to assume that industrial bases can continue to support a long war or that reserve forces can be protected and brought into battle when required. The technologies he discusses are not only those of long-range nuclear-armed ballistic missiles, but also conventional weapons capable of both long range and extreme accuracy.[11] Although not explicitly stated, the logic of this essay brings into question the principle of protraction, for if modern weaponry grants the capability of making deep attacks in the initial offensive, then the chances of successfully conducting a strategy of protraction become slim. Yet another essay argued against placing too much emphasis on the importance of the early stages of a war, arguing that when a country has the capability to sustain a war "the initial stage of a war cannot decide who is the victor or the defeated."[12]

This internal debate may well be continuing, but Chinese analyses of their military exercises over the past several years indicate a commitment to a more forward defense of China, especially in the industrial areas of northeast China. Thus the current strategy requires that positional defense receive greater emphasis than it did in Mao's defensive strategy formulations. Mao Zedong stressed mobility and fluid fronts, but the current strategy demands at least equal emphasis on positional warfare. Indeed, senior commanders have expressed a preference for offensive operations early in the war, but argue that "because of the developments in weapons and technical equipment such a strategy would be difficult to implement."[13] Thus the present approach to defending China appears to be a compromise created by the relatively limited capabilities of the arms and equipment of the Chinese armed forces.

This compromise consists of using the sheer size of the Chinese ground and air forces to cover the most likely avenues of attack with prepositioned forces. The initial attacks will be confronted with defenses in depth designed, especially in mountainous terrain, not so much to block a Soviet offensive as to seriously weaken Soviet forces as they penetrate and pass through Chinese defenses. Ultimately, it is believed that defense in depth combined with mobile warfare conducted by small units will so weaken the logistical support system required to sustain the heavily armored and mechanized Soviet forces that they will become susceptible to counteratack. Counteroffensives conducted by Chinese heavy divisions with close air support and battlefield interdiction sorties will disrupt and block the major axes of the Soviet attack.

Strategy, however, cannot be adequately analyzed without

reviewing the military operations used to support it. Since 1981, the Chinese armed forces have demonstrated considerable concern over their ability to conduct the military operations necessary to successfully fight in the opening stages of a war.[14] They recognize that they must devise concepts of military operations that fit the level of technology they bring to the battlefield. The primary objective over the past seven years has been to improve the capability of the armed forces to conduct combined arms warfare. Combined arms tactics are properly seen as making the most effective use of the forces they now have, and effective execution of these tactics will prepare the PLA for more advanced weaponry as it becomes available. Extensive exercises have been designed and conducted to specifically test the armed forces' ability to wage combined arms warfare in the initial stages of a war.

Although these exercises have been designed primarily for conventional warfare, as early as 1979 the issue of battlefield nuclear weapons was raised. As one analyst defined the problem, "our stiff resistance and repeated counterattacks could make the enemy so frustrated that he might resort to tactical nuclear weapons to spring a shock attack."[15]

In 1982, the Chinese began conducting military exercises in which battlefield nuclear weapons were simulated in the scenarios. Two such exercises were conducted in northern China. In one, Chinese forces were required to respond to an attack in which tactical weapons were used to open up Chinese defensive positions. Paratroops were dropped into the area to take up new defensive positions while helicopters laid antitank munitions to impede any breakthrough attempt by the aggressor's armored forces.[16] In the second exercise, conducted in Ningxia province south of the Mongolian People's Republic, the PLA simulated the use of battlefield nuclear weapons to break up a concentration of enemy forces. For this manuever, the helicopters that brought airmobile forces to the battle area were supported by tanks and close air support sorties as the Chinese sought to use mobility and speed to exploit the shock effect created by the use of nuclear weapons.[17]

It is evident that Chinese strategists have moved far from the concepts of strategy and military operations associated with People's War as it was fought in the 1930s. Military exercises conducted around the use of battlefield nuclear weapons demonstrate the extent to which the Chinese have embraced the objective of disrupting and ejecting a Soviet attack as early as possible. Here there may be a link with Chinese concepts of strategic nuclear deterrence, for as Chinese strategists become more confident in Beijing's ability to deter a nuclear war they may also become more confident that the use of battlefield nuclear weapons will not automatically lead to nuclear war at the strategic level.[18]

Two points must be raised here, both of which are quite speculative. Even though Chinese discussions of strategies and military operations designed to defeat a "future war against aggression" indicate that Beijing's purpose is to fend off a major

Soviet attack designed to seize a major portion of north and northeast China, the ability to conduct effective military operations in the early stages of a war would assist China in developing the capability to defend against more limited Soviet objectives. One possible example of a limited Soviet objective would be a "punitive" expedition similar to that conducted by China into Vietnam. Military exercises in nothern China could possibly fulfill a dual purpose. They are clearly useful as military exercises designed to test the PLA's abilities to conduct combined arms warfare, but they could also be used as a deterrent by demonstrating the PLA's ability to fight effectively in the opening stages of a conflict. This deterrent function could be directed at both levels of warfare; either a limited incursion or a major assault. Yet these kinds of exercises have not been reported from Xinjiang, where China is much more exposed to Soviet attack because so few forces are deployed in the region. It is plausible, however, that given the length of their border with the USSR the Chinese have decided, at least initially, to limit their exercises to those areas where a Soviet attack would have the greatest economic and political effect.

THE PROBLEM OF AIR DEFENSE

Although Chinese strategic and operational analyses generally eschew discussion of air warfare, any investigation of Chinese strategic and doctrinal concepts for a war with the Soviet Union cannot but review the problems faced by their air forces if they are to engage the USSR. With some 5,000 fixed wing combat aircraft and around 100 surface-to-air missile (SAM) units deploying Chinese-built Soviet SA-2 missile systems, it is clear that the Chinese recognize the importance of air power. Similarly, in an essay on naval air forces, a Chinese analyst discussed the importance of controlling air space in order to control the sea. The discussion included analyses of the significance of advances in the technology of modern combat aircraft for achieving air superiority.[19]

Furthermore, China's civil defense program, known originally as "People's Air Defense" but now more often referred to "Civil Air Defense," is very active in creating passive defenses against air attack and is well known for the extensive underground facilities built in many of China's cities. These include stores, theaters, hotels, auditoria, etc., all in daily use, and provide tunnels permitting escape routes from the cities to the surrounding countryside. With their own water supplies, electrical generators, and air filtration systems these extensive shelters are in regular use, but in war they will be used to both defend the civil population and move military forces through tunnel systems, many of which are large enough to accept truck traffic.[20]

The absence of any systematic discussion of the role of air power in China's military strategy is obviously not due to any lack of understanding of the importance of air warfare. In part, it may be due to the dominance of ground force commanders within the Chinese military hierarchy. If Chinese strategic analysis is dominated by the problems faced in conducting a ground war, it may be because the experience of Chinese commanders is primarily in ground warfare. It is also possible that the difficulties the Chinese face in conducting an air war against Soviet forces has reduced public discussion to minimal levels.

The aircraft and ground-based air defense systems employed by the Chinese armed forces would have great difficulty in preventing the USSR from achieving control of the air in either a major war or a limited incursion into China.[21] Soviet forces would use helicopter gunships, close air support, and battlefield interdiction missions to break open Chinese defenses, while bomber forces would be used to destroy railroads, bridges, communication centers, airfields, and logistical support facilities. How successfully Chinese air forces and ground-based air defense weapons could defend against the kind of air power the USSR would use in an attack is highly questionable. If China were planning a traditional People's War, then Soviet air power would not be so threatening. However, Chinese strategists have been planning for a far different war and the success of the strategy is based in large part on combined arms military operations used in the initial stages of the conflict. Indeed, war as it was fought in the 1930s has been declared "absurd" and destined for certain defeat if employed in the 1980s.[22] Yet to engage Soviet forces with an air force incapable of successfully performing its role within the combined arms concepts now being applied to the revised strategy for the defense of China would be to court defeat. It is for this reason that China has shown extreme interest in acquiring advanced avionics and the Hawk surface-to-air missile from the United States.[23]

There is clearly a major weakness in the strategic revision now being formulated to complement the loose concepts associated with the doctrine of People's War under Modern Conditions. Ultimately, the strategy employed has to be implemented by military operations. It is precisely here that technological weaknesses are demonstrated. This is not to say that technology determines the outcome of war, but it does play a major role in the outcome when the strategy requires the application of particular technologies. For a war with the USSR, air power will play a critical role in the strategy being developed and tested by the Chinese armed forces. It could well be, however, that as they test the strategy the Chinese will be able to untangle the most urgently needed technologies from among what must be an extremely long list of desirable but competitive items.

CONCLUSIONS AND SPECULATIONS

The changes that have occurred in Chinese strategic concepts are not the result of major changes in the technological base of the PLA's arms and equipment. They are the result of changes in the way in which Chinese strategists plan to use both the forces they now have and those they seek to develop in the future. It is as if Chinese military thought stagnated in the 1960s and the 1970s, and only since the late 1970s have the Chinese begun to think systematically about what they can do to make the most effective use of the forces they have already deployed.

To some extent the changes may also reflect greater Chinese confidence in their nuclear deterrent as land-based ICBMs and submarine-launched systems reach operational status. Deterrence by "punishment" is becoming more plausible to the Chinese leadership as they gain more confidence in China's second strike capability.[24]

Perhaps more important are the years of training and reorganization that may make the Chinese armed forces more competent to implement a strategy designed to make better use of their current force structure. Although it is difficult to make accurate assessments from this distance, for some six years the Chinese press, journals, and radio broadcasts have been reporting combined arms exercises and it must be assumed some progress has been made. Similarly, Chinese centers of professional military education have been reporting that they are training officers in the techniques of modern warfare. The General Logistics Department reports that improvements are being made in its ability to support intensive warfare. These same reports and articles, written by senior military officials, also note that much remains to be done and that there is yet considerable resistance to the policies designed to modernize the armed forces and improve their effectiveness in fighting modern warfare from those officers who see their status and prestige threatened by the new wave of modernization.[25]

Even with the acknowledged weaknesses in the PLA's modernization program and its military technology, it is quite evident that People's War as it was fought in the 1930s and 1940s was rejected some years ago. Although without a formal statement of China's basic military doctrine it is difficult to determine precisely what doctrinal changes have taken place, it is clear that People's War under Modern Conditions means something quite different from People's War as it was fought by Mao's armies in the 1930s and 1940s.[26] Continued reverence for Mao Zedong's principles of war should not hide the fact that the type of war the Chinese plan to fight will be radically different from that fought by the Red Army of Workers and Peasants. If the analysis in this chapter is correct, then despite the fact that no formal revision of doctrine seems to have been approved, the goal is now to develop the technological capabilities and the professional skills required to make the emerging concepts of strategy and military operations more feasible.

Extending this pattern forward for a decade or more, and assuming a slow but steady improvement in the arms and equipment of the Chinese armed forces, the PLA will be a far more formidable opponent than it is today. There is also an important historical continuity, since, nuclear weapons aside, taking war to the enemy as soon as possible has been the pattern of Chinese military operations since 1949. This was precisely the tactical objective set by China's battlefield commanders in the Korean war, the border war with India, and the 1979 invasion of Vietnam. In each of these conflicts, China argued that its military actions were purely defensive. Yet, on the battlefield, the Chinese went on the offensive taking the war to the "aggressor."

With the USSR, however, Beijing faces an adversary potentially far more dangerous in terms of its ability to sustain a war inside China than any other enemy in the recent past. Nonetheless, China did risk war in 1969 when it fought Soviet troops on a disputed island in the Ussuri River, and Soviet troops deployed along China's northern border did not deter Beijing from invading Vietnam. Reviewing the concepts of strategy and military operations that have emerged from Chinese analyses and field exercises over the past seven years and especially since 1981, it seems evident that China plans to fight in the future as it has in the recent past. The Chinese "way of war" since 1949 has been to take the battle to the "aggressor" at the earliest opportunity. It is, perhaps, within this perspective rather than relying solely on attempts to untangle turgid expositions of Mao Zedong's military thought and Marxism-Leninism that one should analyze the import of China's revisions in its concepts of military strategy.

NOTES

1. The views expressed in this chapter are those of the author and are not to be construed as those of the Department of the Air Force, the Air University, or any other agency of the United States Government.

2. Zhang Aiping, "Several Questions Concerning Modernization of National Defense," Hongqi, no. 5, 1 March 1983, in Foreign Broadcast Information Service China Report (hereafter referred to as FBIS-CHI), no. 053, 17 March 1983, p. K-3.

3. Georges Tan Eng Bok, "Strategic Doctrine," in Gerald Segal and William T. Tow (eds.), Chinese Defense Policy (London: The MacMillan Press, Ltd., 1984), pp. 6-9.

4. Ibid., p. 10.

5. Yang Shangkun, "Steadfastly Uphold and Develop Mao Zedong's Military Thought--Commemorating the 90th Anniversary of the Birth of Mao Zedong," Renmin Ribao, 26 December 1983, in Joint Publication Research Service (henceforth JPRS), China Report, no. 008, 24 January 1984, p. 42.

6. Order of battle information is from The Military Balance 1983-1984 (London: The International Institute for Strategic Studies, Autumn 1983), p. 84.

7. Xu Xiangqian, "Strive to Achieve Modernization in National Defense," Hongqi, no. 10, 2 October 1979, in FBIS-CHI, no. 203, 18 October 1979, p. L-16.

8. Zhang Aiping, "Several Questions," p. K-2.

9. Harlan W. Jencks, "China's 'Punitive War' on Vietnam: A Military Assessment," Asian Survey, vol. 19, no. 8 (August 1979): 801-815.

10. "Nieh Jung-Chan's (Nie Rongzhen) 4 August Speech at the National Militia Conference," Peking (Beijing), NCNA Domestic Service, 7 August 1978, in FBIS-CHI, no. 154, 9 August 1978, p. E-7; and Song Shilun, "Mao's Military Thinking Is the Guide to Our Armies' Victories," Hongqi, no. 16, 16 August 1981, in FBIS-CHI, no. 180, 17 September 1981, p. K-22.

11. Zong He, "Tentative Discussion of the Characteristics of Modern Warfare," Shijie Zhishi, no. 15, 1 August 1983, in JPRS, China Report, no. 461, 11 October 1983, p. 79.

12. Su Jiang, "Unscientific Trends in Military Theory," Zhexue Yanjiu (Philosophical Studies), no. 5 (n.d.), in FBIS-CHI, no. 126, 29 June 1983, p. K-7.

13. Song Shilun, "Mao's Military Thinking," p. K-21.

14. Beijing, Xinhua Domestic Service, 17 January 1982, in FBIS-CHI, no. 12, 19 January 1982, p. K-11.

15. Xu Baoshan, "We Must Be Prepared To Fight Nuclear War in First Stages of Any Future War," Jiefangjun Bao, 16 September 1979, in JPRS, China Report, no. 088, 4 June 1980, p. 99.

16. Beijing Xinhua, 20 July 1982, in FBIS-CHI, no. 141, 22 July 1982, pp. K-2 - K-4.

17. Ningxia Ribao, 28 June 1982, in FBIS-CHI, no. 129, 6 July 1982, pp. K-19 - K-20; and "China Tests New Military Strategy," New York Times, 14 July 1982, p. 3.

18. See Xu Baoshan, "We Must Be Prepared," for his argument in support of this proposition.

19. Li Jing (no title), in Hangkong Zhishi (Aerospace Knowledge), no. 6, June 1983, in JPRS, China Report, no. 008, 24 January 1984, pp. 51-56.

20. See, for example, Drew Middleton, "Vast Air-Raid Shelters Tunnel Under Main Chinese Cities," New York Times, 3 December 1976, p. 1; and Harrison E. Salisbury, "Visitor to Manchuria Finds

Nuclear Shelters Under Construction," <u>New York Times</u>, 25 October 1977, p. 17.

21. For an analysis of the difficulties that would be faced by the Chinese forces in an air war with the USSR, see Bill Sweetman, "Air Forces," in Segal and Tow, <u>Chinese Defense Policy</u>, pp. 71-84.

22. Beijing, Xinhua Domestic Service, 9 September 1979, in FBIS-CHI, no. 176, 10 September 1979, p. L-15.

23. Rick Atkinson, "U.S. Sets First Arms Sales to Peking," <u>Washington Post</u>, 15 June 1984, p. 1.

24. See PLA Deputy Chief of Staff Zhang Zhen's reference to China's "second-strike" capability in an interview with <u>Liaowang</u> reported in FBIS-CHI, no. 147, 30 July 1984, p. K-6; and Gerald Segal, "Nuclear Forces," in Segal and Tow, <u>Chinese Defense Policy</u>, pp. 98-113.

25. See, for example, Yang Shangkun, "Building a Chinese-Style Modernized Armed Forces," <u>Hongqi</u>, no. 15, 1 August 1984, in FBIS-CHI, no. 163, 21 August 1984, pp. K-8 - K-18.

26. Xu Xiangqian, "Strive to Achieve," p. L-16.

2

The Interplay of Science and Technology in Chinese Military Modernization

William T. Tow

The way in which the People's Republic of China (PRC) will link its growing array of sciences and technology (S&T) to its future military modernization is a major factor in resolving that country's strategic destiny. Beijing's current pragmatic leadership faces the challenge of delicately reconciling a national heritage characterized by xenophobia, internecine bureaucratic strife, and ideological factionalization with the necessity to sustain or accelerate the nation's current momentum in acquiring and assimilating the latest "state of the art" military knowledge and weapons components. If the Chinese fail to achieve an admittedly elusive balance between deferring to traditional Sinocentric concerns about compromising sovereign prerogatives through foreign influence with fulfilling the strategic requirements for closing the military technology gap with foreign powers, they will eventually lose a large share of their geopolitical independence to more global strategic actors. The key Chinese task in a strategic sense is therefore to create a formidable indigenous defense infrastructure by gauging their own scientific and economic programs with the overall international trends of technological innovation.[1]

Such hard realities confront China despite its maintaining the world's largest ground forces, a sizable navy and air force, a growing inventory of strategic and theater nuclear forces, and a defense industrial system second in size only to those of the Soviet Union and United States.[2] Indeed, China's progress in defense modernization is most frequently characterized by both official and knowledgeable private Western analysts as "moderate" or "steadily improving but still unspectacular."[3] Many of its current weapons systems reflect unsophisticated 1950s technology largely of Soviet design. Traditional Chinese military production practices have chosen simplicity over more complex Soviet or Western technologies that are on the cutting edge of modern science. As such, the Chinese have tended to favor "quick fix" methods for producing what they perceive to be modern weapons systems rather than forging actual precedents for comprehensive unified defense planning over the long term. At present, China has had little experience in combining its defense and civilian industries in order to eliminate a dual structure of redundant scientific and technological research and development operations that has allowed little technological transfer from one sector to the other. Conspicuous gaps in military communications systems (C^3I), integrated circuit and computer production, advanced battlefield electronics, and engine and air force construction all point to the ramifications of China's past failure to coordinate national research efforts with defense doctrine and management.

In assessing China's prospects for transforming both its strategic and conventional forces into those commensurate with a first-rate military power, several factors appear to be paramount:

-- Modernization vs. bureaucracy. With its current shortage of scientists, engineers, and skilled technicians, will the PRC afford military modernization enough priority in its overall quest for social and economic progress to develop and support a more streamlined defense force than that topheavy institution which the People's Liberation Army (PLA) now reflects? The issue of reconciling the Chinese Communist Party's (CCP's) long-standing ideological ambiguities toward technocrats exercising administrative rights and upward mobility in relation to party cadre or to the traditional military commands is also far from being reconciled.

-- Sovereignty vs. necessary foreign imports. Will China's leaders be able to overcome their society's cultural propensity of always prioritizing the maintenance of national sovereignty over all other considerations? If not, there seems little prospect for the Chinese to keep apace with scientific and technical innovation or to effect the necessary levels of assimilation.

-- Doctrinal assimilation of new systems. Can China's military leadership effectively match their country's military doctrinal precepts with incoming technology and weapons systems? It remains far from clear that China's traditional biases toward applying historical romance, psychology, and deceptions to military problems will be smoothly displaced by an outlook more in line with technological imperatives.[4]

-- Bureaucratic rivalries. The military technology assimilation process itself remains unsettled in China, both from an internal and an external perspective. Internally, rival organizational mechanisms debate over how much outside technology should be introduced into China's backward industrial base, and uncertainty as to how pure research should relate to applied knowledge in the research and development of military capabilities all complicate the S&T matrix as seen by Beijing's leadership. Externally, China's potential suppliers of defense technology remain divided over what restraints should be imposed upon the world's largest communist nation. Strong ideological differences still exist, for example, between the United States and its allies on the one hand and Beijing on the other regarding the fate of Taiwan, the support of violent revolutions in the Third World, and over how the development of market economies should be pursued within a framework of national development.

Determining science and technology's impact on the scope of PLA modernization and costs, resolving the innate contradiction between assimilating outside knowledge and retaining sovereign controls, unifying doctrine with capability, and reconciling internal and external barriers to military-related scientific and technical assimilation are all key challenges with which the Chinese leadership is presently confronted. After reviewing the options and barriers facing China as it emerges within this set of considerations, some brief generalizations will be offered on why China can effect the global military balance if it successfully responds to these challenges.

DEFENSE SCIENTIFIC AND TECHNICAL ADVANCEMENT AS A MODERNIZATION PRIORITY

Since the ten year program for China's Four Modernizations was publicly revealed in 1978, defense improvement and scientific and technical progress have vied for third position (behind agriculture and industry) in the country's overall national modernization efforts. China's military leaders have rationalized this order based on their country's present inability to sustain the multibillion dollar expense of those weapons required for catapulting China's forces into strategic parity with the Soviet Union and the United States. China is, however, determined to match the Soviet and American defensive strength over the long-term by creating the type of indigenous scientific and technological infrastructure needed to produce its own modern weapons. Chinese Defense Minister Xu Xiangqian's landmark October 1979 statement directing current national defense efforts to be undertaken with existing weapon inventories, even as newer ones are developed, has remained the operative policy embraced by China for gradually acquiring the technology necessary for advanced weapons design programs.[5]

What remains unclear is the extent to which China's defense planners have delineated functions and inter-relationships among the several military production efforts within the context of overall national development and budgeting priorities. "Mountaintopism" or "back-door clique behavior" of China's decisionmaking elites who tend to rely on their own political and social networks instead of operating through open party or government channels still comprise an integral part of domestic

Chinese politics, often defying understanding by Western observers.[6] Integrating technological defense modernization elements into a Chinese strategic program designed to deter threats of "modern war" (i.e. highly mechanized Soviet armies deployed across the spectrum of warfare capabilities), will require management reforms in order to supercede the barriers of China's elitism and largely ineffectual bureaucracy.

Initially, better interplay between the national science budget--usually couched under the more general category of "social, cultural, and educational" expenditures--and defense funding will have to be developed. As it is, both pure and applied national research expenditures, either of a military or non-military nature, have declined since the Cultural Revolution. Indeed, China's current underspending in scientific and technical research and development would seem to contradict that country's avowed policy of pursuing a long-term catch-up game with the Soviet Union and the United States.[7] Better resource management and bureaucratic reorganization would go far toward correcting such deficiencies. Reflecting this reality, the Shanghai-based journal, Shijie Jingji Daobao ("World Economic Herald"), recently noted that China must "conscientiously study the condition of the organizational structure and production systems of the European and American countries.... and then ....formulate an outline of development for the early 21st century."[8] What remains unanswered, however, is whether any such raised expectations for enhancing scientific and technical management is within the Four Modernizations rubric or whether it is nothing more than a cynical expediency pursued by the present leadership as a means to retain its own power base.

Secondly, an emerging generation of professional elites, distinguished by its understanding and applying foreign science and technology, seems uncertain as to what role it will play in China's future. The leadership's current emphasis on technical competence as a primary criterion for upward mobility is by no means a lasting indication that China's young technocrats will always fare well as the party struggles to adjust to changing conditions without undermining its basic principles of socialism, proletarian dictatorship, party leadership, and Marxist-Leninist-Mao Zedong thought. Inevitably, the "cadre-scientists" who gained their positions at China's universities and research institutes at times when ideological purity and "volunteerism" counted for far more than one's technical education will resist widespread pragmatist trends to replace or retire them. Even Deng Xiaoping has admitted to the existence of this problem in a recent interview with Western journalists:

> Questioner: In our contacts with some small groups in China, we have learned that members of these groups believe that some people are not opposed to the general idea of modernization but that if it creates difficulty for their jobs, they will resist it. This means that bureaucracy will obstruct China's modernization.

> Deng: This problem indeed exists. Besides, there are also problems with ideas of privilege, disrespect for science, overconcentration of power and others, which we have already pointed out and want gradually to correct.[9]

A third concern about science and technology's relationship to military affairs is how the Army's "veteran officer corps" will respond to the latest series of government directives calling for the integration of research and development efforts by the civilian and military communities. Will the remaining "Long Marchers" or their subordinates cling to perceived vested interests at the expense of moving toward cooperation with the civilians? Some evidence of military resistance still surfaces on occasion as evidenced by recent <u>Jiefangjun Bao</u> (<u>Liberation Army Daily</u>) and <u>Renmin Ribao</u> (<u>People's Daily</u>) articles. In May 1984, these publications quoted Deng, leader of both the nation's governmental and Party military oversight committees, when he attacked "certain commands in the army" for attempting to "corrode" party directives concerning military modernization. Deng's open criticism of the Army was inevitably unpopular with many of that institution's elites, accustomed to relating with pride the military's traditional role in nation-building and still reeling from the cold fact that defense modernization remains at the bottom of China's development priorities.[10] Even during the early 1960's, in the aftermath of the Army's suppression at the Lushan Plenum, Lin Biao managed to uphold an acceptable "modus vivendi" between Party and military factional interests in ways which the current emphasis on science and technology has yet to achieve. Assuredly, Deng has extended some carrots to the PLA to counterbalance his predominant stick of maintaining a hardline approach against PLA autonomy. These measures have included replacing civilian bureaucrat Geng Biao with military veteran Zhang Aiping as Defense Minister and by conducting more extensive military exercises as well as public displays of PLA inventories on national holidays.[11] It would be premature, however, to conclude that civil-military differences are about to be reconciled to a point where defense-related science and technology can readily span both sectors or to assume that no real divisions between the civilians and the army will materialize during a post-Deng leadership crisis.

SCIENCE AND TECHNOLOGY AND THE SOVEREIGNTY PROBLEM

From 1977 to 1982, the PLA's General Political Department (GPD) served as a self-appointed watchdog over Deng's Four Modernization programs to ensure that economic planning conformed as much as possible to the orthodox tenets of Maoist revolutionary theory. Foremost among the GPD's concerns was that the inviolability of the Chinese nation be preserved, unfettered by foreign domination. In a move to depoliticize the PLA and to force its ideological zealots into compliance to the ruling pragamtists' modernization blueprints for defense as well as for other areas of development, however, the party's Twelfth Party Congress removed Wei Guoqing as head of the GPD in September 1982. Wei had proven unable to prevent the PLA press organs from taking too independent a line from party dictums. He was replaced by Yu Qiuli who has since modified the PLA's resistance to accepting outside scientific and technical assistance.[12]

Simultaneously, the PLA was strikingly ineffective in lobbying for more military funding (from 1977 to 1984, the military's percentage of the total national budget declined from 17.9% to 13.1%) or in establishing any real checks and balances to curb what it deemed to be the pragmatists' zealous tendencies to assimilate foreign knowledge and goods. Such a tendency can be directly attributed to the PLA's (as well as other key internal organ's) perceptions of how rapidly advanced technology can be absorbed into China's own defense infrastructure. This somewhat schizophrenic self-image as a military power and how it related to the technological importation question was perhaps best illustrated by a 1982 essay published by the major party organ Hongqi:

> ...with our strong national defense forces, we are strong enough to defend the peaceful construction of our people ....to maintain our correct foreign policies, we enjoy high political prestige in the world.... but ....our source of funds are, after all limited....
> ....we should not distort self-reliance by closing our country to international exchange and fighting in isolation as "self-reliant"....

The article concluded that there were five types of technological imports which were critical to China's future military and national survival: (1) advanced equipment and equipment components; (2) "new and fine quality" materials which could then be "studied" by Chinese technicians and reproduced internally; (3) adopting new principles relating to management and production; (4) assimilating selective foreign "data and knowhow;" and (5) applying such data and knowhow to "scientific rules of operation."[13]

Under such guidelines, the PLA has clearly been instructed by China's pragmatic leadership to modernize in the most cost-efficient way possible. This instruction encouraged the military's aspirations for achieving long-term self-reliance in defense while supplementing current Chinese military deficiencies through careful selections of foreign military weapons technology. To facilitate this policy, the party has moved to consolidate the Machine Building Industries traditionally run by the army into combined military-civilian production boards. It has created new committees such as the State Commission of Science, Technology, and Industry for National Defense (NDSTIC) to ease the military into a leaner national strategic decisionmaking infrastructure. Defense Minister Zhang Aiping, himself a former chairman of the old National Defense Science and Technology Commission, referred to it as the new, definitive body responsible for the "development, experimentation, and production of foreign and domestic modernized defense equipment for all of the PLA." The Commission's military arm, Zhang surmised, would be staffed by "younger and really promising persons" succeeding "our old comrades who, although experienced, are, after all, old...." Zhang further argued during his announcement that science and technology are constantly advancing and the "knowledge in our possession is not sufficient to cope with them."[14]

In a sense, Deng, Zhang, and their cohorts have attempted to induce modernization within the PLA in a way which that force was not able to do itself. Assuredly, pockets of resistance to the pragmatists' exhortations still exist. For example, the heavy industrial sector has resented defense budget cutbacks following Lin Biao's downfall because output has failed to keep up due to outmoded plant capacities. Additionally, various regional or district military commands are still resisting equipment releases from their commands because eventual replacements may be too complex for the average Chinese peasant military conscript to operate.[15] The present Chinese leaders also recognize that their nation's sovereignty will not necessarily be permanently compromised by imparting some advanced weapons systems in finished form or, conversely, enhanced by pursuing "quick fix" methods (i.e. reverse engineering or cannibalization) to copy such systems. Zhang has observed, after all, that if the PLA is content only on copying "we will only fall behind others....the fundamental way is to rely on ourselves."[16]

Another important dimension to the issues is how China responds to Western efforts to regulate flows of technology on the basis of China's foreign policy and strategic behavior toward the Soviet Union and the Third World. China tends to view American pressures on Beijing to comply with international nuclear proliferation restraints as unwarranted interference with its sovereignty, especially when such compliance is cited by Washington as a pre-condition for approving agreements.[17] China also interprets the U.S. policy of adhering to "evenhanded" weapons transfer formulae as they relate to itself and Taiwan as hypocritical insofar as the Americans have already recognized the principles of "one China" in the 1972 Shanghai Communique. In essence, not only do China's pragmatists face the problem of reconciling their nation's own sovereign traditions and institutions with a more effective absorptive capacity for "things foreign," but they must also simultaneously and carefully assert their interpretation of sovereignty on oft recalcitrant U.S. and other would-be technological suppliers without alienating them in the process.

SCIENCE AND TECHNOLOGY AND CHINESE STRATEGIC DOCTRINE

Notwithstanding the continued U.S. propensity to sell conventional arms to Taiwan, the Soviet threat remains the paramount concern of Chinese military planners. The nature of this threat more closely conforms with traditional strategy faithfully adhered to by the proponents of classical Maoist strategy, many of whom are still within the Chinese miltary command structure.[18] A factor of equal weight, however, is that the West has become China's only real source for the modern weapons technology needed to respond credibly to the Soviet military challenge. As Paul Godwin has concluded: "....the PRC's continued espousal of "People's War under Modern Conditions" represents not only a reluctance to depart from Mao's concepts of strategic defense, but also a recognition that some of the underlying principles of "People's War" do remain applicable to the military threat posed by the Soviet Union...."[19]

How, then, has China attempted to reconcile the military technology question into its overall strategic outlook? It is clear that Beijing sees any future Sino-Soviet conflict as a protracted one which will be fought defensively on Chinese soil. The Army must gradually develop supporting strategies and tactics for building an active defense ("jiji fangyu") through the use of hit-and-run tactics and selective strikes along exterior lines ("wai xian"). Such tactics would be applicable to vast areas of Chinese territory and demand the quick shifting of China's defensive forces in an effort to prevent Soviet troops from invading Xinjiang, Manchuria, or other strategic areas. Avoiding Soviet execution of battlefield surprise or the Soviet Union's effective perpetration of combat superiority through technological means ("voornzhenien"), and disrupting its command and control are all important components of any such Chinese defense. Positional warfare, in the classical Western sense, would play little or no role in this strategy, but selected Western technology could be adapted for strengthening China's defensive credibility. China's Academy of Military Science, for example, is reported to be weighing how the "unified battlefield" approach incorporating electronic warfare (with an emphasis on close combat firing, synchronized fire support, and precisely integrated C^3I) can be incorporated into the types of combat maneuvers most closely associated with traditional Army defensive operations.

The prohibitive costs of extensive conventional defense modernization for the Army, estimated between $300-400 billion to raise the standard to the NATO level, make inevitable the Chinese attempts to minimize their deficiencies by merging a few selected aspects of modern warfare into a minimum deterrent. The fusion of electronics warfare and nuclear technology stands out as a probable key element in this general strategic approach.[20] As such, modern technology is incorporated into Chinese deterrence and defense postures with a maximum sense of flexibility, ranging between self-reliance and foreign purchase, between hypothetical situations of limited war and general war, and between offensive and defensive military actions within an overall People's War context. Inculcation of updated technology into the Army's missions and force inventories can be intermittent, gauged to enhance deterrent capabilities applicable to China's "empty spaces" to the north and west of the country, and to foster eventual self-reliance in the production of such weapons systems.21

Achieving strategic doctrinal credibility through the most cost-effective ways possible seems to be the operative guideline in China's technological outlook. As Yu Qiuli, the head of the PLA's General Political Department, characterized the problem, military capabilities and logistics are best gained through exerting "maximum legitimacy over limited funds" within the overall constraints related to "the nature of war and the desires of the people." Under such conditions, Yu concluded China would move to "rely on its own efforts" in developing modern armaments because it could not afford to buy all the weapons it needed from foreigners and "...(e)ven if we could afford it, it is hard to acquire really advanced weapons of military value."22

If the Chinese failed to prevent a superpower attack on China, "total war" would then become the operative principle in the Chinese strategic outlook. Here, swift destruction of enemy targets at an initial stage of battle, maneuvering along unified lines, upgrading of stockpiles, weapons maintenance and reinforcement, and strengthening command and control through better intelligence, reconnaissance, and electronics capabilities, would be emphasized. Recent Chinese strategic writings have stressed all these factors as emerging characteristics in modern warfare.23 Yet there is little public evidence of extensive attempts to identify those indigenous Chinese military capabilities, which can best be used to fulfill these prerequisites. Recent patterns of Chinese military behavior and technological acquisition can be diagnosed as a vague and unfocused series of efforts by the leadership to revise the country's strategic perception and blueprints.

Nulcear deterrence, by way of illustration, has recently been addressed through establishing a separate strategic missile wing--although what relationship this wing has with the Second Artillery, which was China's original strategic missile element, remains uncertain. China also has concentrated on building up its nuclear-powered ballistic missile-equipped submarine force. The new land-based missile wing, formed during mid-1984, was justified by an Army spokesman as a necessary step due to the "rapid advances in military technology" predicating the need for China "to raise its nuclear attack capability."24 In this sense, the Chinese have acknowledged their need to master a critical requirement of modern warfare: fusing conventional tactical firepower and C^3I with nuclear components for modern warfare conditions.

A related problem confronting the PLA's central authorities is how best to allot tactical nuclear weapons and delivery systems to the regional commanders, heretofore unaccustomed to compliantly accepting directives from the national command authority.25 From the outset of any battle, the enemy's warfighting capability and strategic targets must be destroyed by such Chinese regional deployments as part of an "active defense" component of People's War: attrition and annihilation of China's wartime opponents through resistance against frontal attacks by combined nuclear and conventional counterattacks against the opponents' homelands. Such Chinese nuclear retaliation will inevitably involve the completion of highly sophisticated targeting and communications missions, including the synchronous firing of (land-based and sea-based) ballistic missiles, coordinating advanced telecommunications and computer networks, and using related technology which is now available to China only through Western sources.

If China succeeds in acquiring such defense technology, most reasonable Western estimates surmise that by 1990 Beijing could be controlling around 150 multiple, independently targeted (MIRVed) strategic nuclear delivery vehicles, which would provide it with a significant minimum nuclear deterrent against either the Soviet Union or the United States.[26]

From a warfighting perspective, both the Chinese and their most likely antagonist in a general conflict, the Soviet Union, focus on the importance of protracted war and readiness for post-nuclear phases of warfare. In 1978, then Chinese Defense Minister Xu Xiangqian contended that "People's War under Modern Conditions" meant that even while an enemy may have a decidedly superior edge in nuclear armaments and military technology at the outset of battle, China would be successful in building up rear area strategic bases to support a prolonged conflict following the enemy's initial attack.[27]

The notion of protracted war has been ingrained into the Chinese consciousness since 1938 when Mao Zedong first expounded his theories on this subject at Yenan. Territory, human and natural resources, and political cohesion were characterized as variables of equal weight to superior weapons technology for determining the eventual outcome of any conflict fought on Chinese soil. With such thinking, Mao contended, the permanent subjugation of his country could never occur. Instead a war of national resistance would be adopted against any invader. Such a war could only be protracted in nature, with a well-planned strategic territorial defense gradually giving way to counter-offensives designed to secure the aggressor's total defeat.[28]

Recent Chinese strategic writings, however, are placing increased emphasis on the _initial_ stages of modern warfare as the primary determinants for the eventual outcome. This stress is based on the development of new weapons, the recognized utility of strategic surprise, and the enlarged geographic scope, as well as reduced time spans now inherent in conflicts at strategic levels. At least some Chinese military literature in the PRC is now openly concluding that such factors "....indicate that in modern warfare, the battles in the initial stage will play a more important role than ever before in winning the initiative of the war and in its later development."[29]

What remains questionable is the extent to which China can incorporate the technology necessary to allow it to compete on equal terms at the outset of strategic conflict. Such a prospect seems remote as long as China's military modernization program continues to be relegated to last place under the current plan for pursuing China's Four Modernizations economic development program. The fiscal price for attaining those strategic and conventional weapons systems in sufficient quantities is perhaps intolerably high, considering China's present economic base. Conversely, if Beijing were to pursue a great power military posture too rapidly, then the Soviet Union could again consider pre-empting Chinese weapons sites and production centers. During 1969-71, it contemplated such pre-emption (it was forstalled only by stern U.S. warnings and by lukewarm support on the part of its Warsaw Pact allies). Undue tensions caused by a rapid Chinese strategic buildup would also negate the long-term benefits otherwise accorded by gradually assimilating the costs of a military buildup in conjunction with strengthening the nation's economic resilience.

The current development programs would certainly be more difficult to sustain under such circumstances, as would the preferred policy of maintaining a balanced approach between strategic self-reliance and strategic interdependence with other anti-Soviet forces around the world. As Thomas Robinson has speculated, the Soviets may feel compelled to widen the gap of strategic capabilities between their own forces and the PLA and the result could be a ".... China even more beholden to foreign assistance and military ties than is now the case."[30]

The safer middle ground for China's military force planners would be to continue developing relatively cheaper regional, "war-fighting" nuclear components in the form of intermediate-range ballistic missiles (IRBMs)--primarily the CSS-2--in lieu of a much more costly and more risky array of modern conventional forces and exotic nuclear systems. But the axioms of People's War and protracted warfare have actually compelled the Chinese to move toward development of "state-of-the-art" nuclear and conventional military weapons in anticipation of fighting in a post-nuclear milieu, complete with second-strike capabilities and intact command systems. As one Western observer has characterized the Chinese situation: "Maoist doctrine continues to be relevant, rooted in the geopolitical nature of China herself."[31]

CHINA'S SCIENTIFIC AND TECHNICAL RESEARCH AND ASSIMILATION: FACTORS OF INTERNAL DEBATE AND EXTERNAL CONTROLS

Debate among Chinese leaders over acquiring foreign military technology can be traced back to Soviet material and technological assistance between 1953 and 1959. Closely preceding Stalin's death in 1952, two machine-building minstries were created, one to produce civilian goods and the other to manufacture arms. The Soviet Union provided technology transfer agreements which called for shipping heavy industrial equipment and facilities to China. By the end of the decade, over 150 whole-plant projects were supported with Soviet assistance, some 11,000 Soviet technicians had been directly involved in plant start-ups and in related projects, and approximately 25,000 Chinese had been sent to the Soviet Union for advanced education and technical training.

Succinctly, the Soviets, who had largely shaped the development of China's production and scientific and technical infrastructures, presented China's leaders with a devastating lesson in self-reliance when they left China in 1960 as a result of ideological and diplomatic rifts.[32]

While China continues to tilt unmistakably toward principles of self-reliance in military technology assimilation, several factors have worked to mitigate the PRC's complete adherence to self-sufficiency in military technology development. First, Beijing recognizes that while it struggles to narrow the scientific and technical "learning curve" with more developed nations, the rest of the world is moving toward new and more exotic weapons systems, thereby widening the curve in relation to China's own capabilities. Secondly, advanced countries retain or increase their leading edge in the industrial and civilian research sectors which have obvious "spill-over" effects on a national military capacity.[33] In many cases, China can achieve access to the latest technologies only through entering into licensing and co-production arrangements with Western industrial countries on conditions which preclude a high level of Chinese xenophobia. In fact, since the early 1970s, China has entered into agreements with these nations at a rate which far exceeded the Soviet experience. In this way, it has gained access to the international pool of technical knowledge for purposes related to its own national development needs, including military modernization. China's overall history of tapping foreign expertise has been ably summarized by Dennis Fred Simon:

> '....a pattern of alternating shifts bewween periods of extreme self-reliance and selective foreign borrowing.... as a result of political competition between two major groups in China ....,' the radical economic nationalists and those favoring economic intercourse with outside forces, resulting in '....the uneven pattern of industrial growth that has characterized the Chinese economy over the past 30 years.'[34]

Currently, as several respected Western analysts have noted, China could opt for one of two military courses.[35] The first policy direction would be China's emulation of the United States, Soviet Union, and Gaullist France in its determination to use national research and development efforts for heightening its prestige within the global community. An alternative approach would anticipate continued predominance of China's economists and civilian technocrats in society and their adoption of a "gradualist" national movement, ear-marking newly acquired market development and long-term investment planning, a la Japan. China's decision to lift centralized price controls and to reduce state economic planning in October 1984 indicates that Deng and his pragmatist counterparts have prevailed over countervailing movements favoring accelerated military expenditures at the expense of scientific and technical development related to the other sectors.36

In essence, the PLA has apparently accepted the prospect of buying only a few weapon systems to correct the major deficiencies against the current Soviet threat. It thus has most likely endorsed the activities of such bodies as the Chinese Working Group, Sino-American Military Technical Cooperation Negotiations, and other Chinese delegations now bargaining with West European defense firms.37 The quid pro quo for such acquiesence by the military, however, is that it will, over time, be increasingly strident in its demands for greater resource allocations. It matters little to the PLA whether these demands are met through scientific and technical spillovers from other sectors (the pragmatists' preferred outcome) or through increased purchases of more expensive weapon systems from abroad.

To a great extent, the ultimate path will be determined by external factors over which China may have limited control. The case of the Coordinating Committee of the Consultative Group on export controls to communist nations (COCOM) is illustrative in this regard. Japan and many European COCOM members often have been reluctant to approve Chinese military purchases from the United States, for example, for fear of antagonizing the Soviet Union, against which COCOM still exercises comparatively more tightened controls.38 However the recent reclassification of China on the U.S. Munitions Control List has exacerbated the problem. Beijing is now classified as a "friendly power," which complicated COCOM planning because the U.S. criteria have to be matched with COCOM's own lists relating to military items, atomic energy, and high technology industrial items that may have "dual use" (military/-civilian) application.39

In July 1984, the dilemma posed by this "China differential" among the Western allies was highlighted when COCOM officials announced new measures to significantly tighten controls over the export of advanced computer components to the Soviet bloc. No consensus had been successfully reached, however, on whether to apply such controls to China and, if so, how to apply them.40 As procedures now stand, lengthy delays often occur and at least some COCOM members bypass the committee's channels by selling material through backdoor channels in Hong Kong. The United States has concluded that COCOM is underfunded, understaffed, and undersupported which, in turn, tends to create an ad hoc control system which China can manipulate to its advantage. However, it appears that Western controls may soon be tightened. Any such restriction would be viewed by Beijing as an infringement on its own "sovereign right" to acquire science and technology in the international market place.

More likely, both China and the West will realize the benefits of maintaining a laissez faire posture toward the trade and technology transfer issue, at least for the near term. If this occurs, then political relations could be strengthened in ways which could temper the desires of either side to deal with Moscow. The West could also assume that the same interrelated economic and social patterns which drew Japan into the Western orbit after World War II could exercise a similar pull on China's pragmatists who are now seeking out highly beneficial market relationships. Technology transfer can be a long-term instrument of national persuasion for those dealing with China. This belief is supported by Beijing's continued inclination to reap the benefits of the 1979 and 1984 U.S.-Chinese Science and Technology Agreements. The influence of technology, moreover, might ease the occasional aggravation in Sino-American relations caused by Taiwan and by conflicting Sino-American policies toward the Third World. Technology could also soften the ideological schisms between Chinese and Western societies insofar as both can point to positive aspects of the technology flow as either justifying a post-Maoist variant of orthodox Marxism--or a phenomenon which tends to lure a Marxist state toward a more capitalist path.[41] The absence of a Western consensus on technology transfer to China may prevent the realization of such benefits if China's export control policy becomes directed toward Moscow, if the present controls are flaunted by the West, or if short-term commercial gains supercede the West's ability to forge a more enduring alliance.

THE GEOPOLITICAL OUTLOOK

Many Western strategic planners foresee a gradual evolution in Sino-Western collective defense ties, strong enough to contain Moscow's military activities in the Far East in ways which other regional anti-Soviet alliance systems could never do. However, other Asian-Pacific nations are less enthusiastic about such prospects. ASEAN leaders, for example, have sharply resisted U.S. arguments about the strategic benefits of allowing Beijing access to Western technology. They point out that a stronger China would be capable militarily of threatening Southeast Asian security by challenging the growing Soviet power there or by supporting insurgent movements more effectively than it did during the era of decolonization two decades ago.[42] The possibility that either China or Japan will embark on a major military modernization program is a great problem for other Asian states but most of all for the Soviet Union. Most of Soviet territory straddles the Asian continent and Moscow has warned repeatedly that continued U.S. or Western military-related sales to China will eventually become a "high military risk" both to the West and China.[43] Such a threat seems less potent in light of the fact that Deng Xiaoping's economic modernization programs are specifically geared toward making China a first-rank, <u>independent</u>, and <u>non-aligned</u> power, equidistant from both the Soviet Union and the United States. While China still fears Soviet military power more than U.S. forces, it seems prudent to recall that the Chinese Communist ideologue of good standing still remains wary of the West's economic and political system as well.

When China attempts to buy technology directly related to its strategic missile programs, ground and air defenses, and armored mobility, the United States may be forced to revise its now confident estimates that high technology transfers to China can be controlled to the West's benefit. In fact, statements such as those recently attributed to Presidential Science Advisor George Keyworth that "facilitating China's missile trajectory calculations hardly compromises our own strategic interests," would seem to be, at least, premature and short-sighted.[44] The Reagan Administration must avoid making the same mistake that the Soviet Union made during the 1950s when it assumed that it was possible to transfer technology to China so discriminately that Beijing would not be able to develop a threatening military capability.

It would be well for the West to keep in mind that regardless of how China finally decides to integrate foreign technology into its military modernization efforts, the <u>national</u> dimension of any Chinese strategic policy will continue to be emphasized by Chinese decisionmakers. Visions of China's conforming to the visions of U.S. strategists favoring closer Sino-U.S. military ties on the basis of building a new anti-Soviet collective defense system are not likely to be fulfilled. Above all, China's leaders are convinced that modern defense technology must ultimately fit into the PLA's mission of preserving China's revolutionary traditions and responding to "national conditions" of culture, ideology, and politics. Within such a framework, the goal of self-reliance seems not only logical but absolutely essential to the objectives of the Chinese state. Yet China's self-perceived historical roots do at times clash with what its leadership recognizes as a new "international situation." In this setting, China's lack of technological proficiency will leave it unable to solve a host of domestic political, managerial, and logistical challenges.

How well China can manipulate the interplay of modern strategy and technology with regard to its own potential for becoming a world power by the end of this century will be largely determined by how well Chinese pragmatists neutralize domestic conservatives' resistance to those external sources best able to provide China the future instruments of power. In turn, the United States and its allies need to upgrade their own efforts in forging common strategies directed toward modernizing China without arming it in ways which could ultimately compromise their own security and global stability.

NOTES

1. See especially the observations of Dennis Fred Simon, "The Role of Science and Technology in China's Foreign Relations," <u>China and The World</u>, ed. Samuel S. Kim (Boulder, CO: Westview Press, 1984), pp. 293-318.

2. U.S. Central Intelligence Agency analyst Sydney James has asserted, for example, that China has indeed advanced further toward military self-sufficiency than has any other Third World state, with its overall defense industry now ranking as the third largest in the world after the United States and Soviet Union and

producing a formidably wide range of weapon systems. See James, "Military Industry," Chinese Defense Policy, ed. Gerald Segal and William T. Tow (Urbana and Chicago: University of Illinois Press, 1984), p. 117.

3. The Organization of the Joint Chiefs of Staff, United States Military Posture For FY 1983 (Washington, DC: U.S. Government Printing Office, 1982), pp. 42-43. Official U.S. estimates of Chinese military spending trends are found in the testimony of Lt. Gen. James A. Williams, Director, Defense Intelligence Agency (DIA), in Hearings before the Subcommittee on International Trade, Finance, and Security Economics of the Joint Economics Committee, U.S. Congress, Allocation of Resources in the Soviet Union and China--1982 97th Cong., 2nd Sess., 29 June 1982, pp. 49, 104. Other estimates are provided by Research Institute for Peace and Security (Tokyo), Asian Security 1982 (Tokyo: RIPS, 1982), p. 76, and by Leonard Sullivan, Jr. with Ellen L. Frost and David S. Holland, "Trade and Technology Transfers," in Report of The Atlantic Council's Committee on China Policy, China: Policy for the Next Decade (Boston: Oelgeschlager, Gunn & Hain, Publishers, Inc., 1984), pp. 310-311.

4. Note the comments of Jonathan Pollack, "Rebuilding China's Great Wall: Chinese Security in the 1980s," The China Defense Establishment, ed. Paul H. B. Godwin (Boulder, CO: Westview, 1983), pp. 17-18.

5. Harlan W. Jencks lends the most cogent analysis of this trend in From Muskets to Missiles (Boulder, CO: Westview, 1982), pp. 151-152. Also see the analysis of recent statements by Deng Xiaoping concerning the adequacy of China's minimum nuclear deterrent for "buying time" in Christopher M. Clarke, "Defense Modernization," The China Business Review (July-August 1984): 40-41; and Harvey W. Nelson, "Internal Management in the Armed Forces: Confucian Anachronism or Model for the 1980s?" in Godwin, pp. 141-145.

6. An exceptional Western analysis of this problem, however, is Jurgen Domes, "Intra-Elite Group Formation and Conflict in the PRC," in Groups and Politics in the People's Republic of China, ed. David S. G. Goodman (Armonk, NY: M. E. Sharpe, Inc., 1984), pp. 28-37. Domes contends that some key indications can be employed for recognizing intra-elite divergence from established government policies: terminological divergencies in party propaganda lines adopted by party or government organs under a particular elite's control; the removal of specific elites from various party or governmental positions without the evoking of their party memberships; or, on a more extreme basis, expulsion of certain elites from the party and the emergence of open rifts between elites.

7. For background, consult Richard P. Suttmeier, "'Moon-Ghetto' Problems in China's Alternative Scientific Futures," China: The 80s Era, ed. Norton Ginsberg and Bernard Lalor (Boulder, CO: Westview Press, 1984), pp. 304-308.

8. Qian Xuesen, "On Understanding The New Scientific Revolution," Shijie jingji daobao (World Economic Herald), 19 April 1984, as reprinted in Joint Publications Research Service (JPRS), 84-019, China Report-Science & Technology, 27 June 1984, p. 12.

9. Interview of Deng Xiaoping by the Christian Science Monitor as reprinted in Foreign Broadcast Information Service (FBIS), China Daily Report 24 November 1980, p. C-20. Also see the comments of Leo A. Orleans, "Education, Careers, and Social Status," and Thomas Fingar, "Consequences of Catching Up," in a special section on Science and Technology in China, Bulletin of the Atomic Scientists 40 (October 1984): 115-165.

10. "Enhance Party Spirit, Eliminate Factionalism," Jiefangjun Bao, 8 May 1984, as translated and reprinted in FBIS, China Daily Report, 9 May 1984, pp. K-14, K-15; "Building the Third Echelon Is a Strategic Task," Jiefangjun Bao, 5 May 1984, as translated and reprinted in FBIS China Daily Report, 7 May 1984, pp. K-11, K-12; and Colina MacDougall, "Peking Leadership Offers a Sop to China's Army After a Series of Public Rebukes," Financial Times, 12 June 1984, p. 3.

11. This point is well illustrated by Gerald Segal, "The Military as a Group in Chinese Politics," in Goodman, pp. 87-88.

12. Richard D. Nethercut, "Deng and the Gun: Party-Military Relations in the PRC," Asian Survey (August 1982): 691-704; and Nethercut, "Leadership in China: Rivalry, Reform and Renewal," Problems of Communism, (March- April 1983): 30-46.

13. "On Questions Regarding our Country: Economic Relations with Foreign Countries," Hongqi (Red Flag), No. 8, 16 April 1982, as translated and reported in FBIS, China (Daily Report), 11 May 1982, p. K-4 - K-11.

14. "Zhang Aiping On Seniority, Other Reform Topics," Xinhua, 27 January 1983, reprinted in FBIS, China Daily Report, 31 January 1983, pp. K-6, K-7.

15. The author is indebted to Christopher M. Clarke for originally raising these observations for consideration.

16. "Zhang Aiping On National Defense Modernization," Zhongguo Xinwen She (New China News Agency) report, 28 February 1983, translated by Foreign Broadcast Information Service (FBIS), China Daily Report, 1 March 1983, pp. K-8, K-9; and "Zhang Aiping

Speaks on Defense Modernization," Xinjua, 28 February 1983, reprinted in FBIS, 2 March 1983, pp. K-5, K-6. Also see Hongqi, 5 (1 March 1983): 21-24, translated by JPRS 83318, China Report, 22 April 1983, pp. 33-39. For a Western assessment, see Robert Delfs, "Swords Into Bicycles," Far Eastern Economic Review 121 (25 August 1983): 91-92.

17. See Don Oberdorfer's incisive report, "Nuclear Pact With China Is Stalled in U.S." International Herald Tribune, 16/17 July 1984, p. 1.

18. This point is ably expanded upon by Banning N. Garrett and Bonnie S. Glaser in War and Peace: The Views of Moscow and Beijing (Berkeley, CA: Institute of International Studies, 1984), especially pp. 120-130. Their analysis relies heavily on writings by analysts with the Beijing Institute for Strategic Studies.

19. Godwin, "Mao Zedong Revised: "Deterrence and Defense in the 1980s," in Godwin, p. 22. There has been little real deviation in Chinese strategic doctrine since the publication of a definitive Jiefangjun Bao article entitled "Problems of Strategy in China's Revolutionary War," largely written by Mao and appearing in Peking Review 10 (13 January 1967): 14-18. Most tellingly, this article contended that "....(n)o matter how modern weapons and technical equipment may advance and how complex modern warfare may be, People's War always remains our most effective weapon...," p. 14.

20. For a definitive PRC Academy of Military Science study on technological needs, see Xitonggongcheng lilun yu shijian (Systems Engineering - Theory and Practice), no. 2, 1983, p. 1 as reprinted in Joint Publications Research Service (JPRS) 84439, China Report, no. 460, 29 September 1983, pp. 92-93. For a Western assessment of Chinese interest high technology warfare studies, see Tony Walker, "China Studies Lessons of Falklands Electronics Warfare," Financial Times, 6 August 1982, p. 3, and "Chinese Officers Study New Warfare," The Japan Times, 19 January 1982, p. 4.

21. These points are especially well developed by Alfred D. Wilhelm, Jr., "National Security-The Chinese Perspective," in Sullivan, et. al., pp. 205-208, 212-215.

22. Interview with Yu Qiuli, "Modernization of National Defense and Building of the People's Army," Beijing Review 26 (1 August 1983): pp. 14, 15.

23. For example, see a remarkable document written by Zong He, a researcher for the Beijing International Strategic Problems Society, entitled "Tentative Discussion on the Characteristics of Modern Warfare," in Shijie zhishi (World Knowledge), no. 15, 1 August 1983 and translated in JPRS 84508, China Report, no. 461, 11 October 1983, pp. 78-88, which addresses all of these strategic

considerations in relatively sophisticated terms by Western standards.

24. "PLA Forms Missile Group," China Daily, 13 June 1984, p. 4.

25. Gerald Segal, "China's Nuclear Posture for the 1980s," Survival 23 (January/February 1981): 15.

26. Analysis of China's developing an SSBN deterrent is offered by Bradley Hahn, "China in the SLBM Club," Pacific Defense Reporter 10 (February 1984): 1720, and David G. Muller, Jr., China as a Maritime Power (Boulder, CO: Westview Press, 1983), pp. 172-175, 225-227. Hahn asserts that China felt the "absolute necessity" to obtain direct Western European, U.S., and Japanese technical support for building its own strategic naval programs before the end of this century while Muller cites a 1979 issue of Jianchuan zhishi (Naval and Merchant Ships) which speculates about second strike nuclear deterrence capabilities of Chinese SSBNs in the event that Chinese land-based nuclear forces became neutralized.

27. Xu Xiangqian, "Heighten Our Vigilance and Get Prepared to Fight a War," Honggi (Red Flag), August 1978 as analyzed by Garrett and Glaser, pp. 126-128.

28. Mao Zedong, Selected Works II (Beijing: Foreign Languages Press, 1975), especially pp. 133-145.

29. Zong He, p. 79.

30. Thomas W. Robinson's testimony in U.S. Congress, Joint Economic Committee, China Under the Four Modernizations - Part I, (Washington, DC: U.S. Government Printing Office, 1982), p. 591.

31. Segal, p. 13.

32. For background on the Sino-Soviet scientific and technical relationships following Mao Zedong's ascension to power, see Simon, "China's Absorption of Foreign Technology: Prospects and Problems," in Ginsberg and Lalor, pp. 328-329; as well as Daniel Wagner and David G. Barlow, "National Defense," in China: A Country Study, ed. Frederica M. Bunge and Rinn-Sup Shinn (Washington, DC: The American University Foreign Area Studies, Spetember 1980), especially pp. 494-495.

33. These arguments are weighed in sophisticated terms by Jon Sigurdson, Technology and Science in the People's Republic of China (Oxford, New York, Toronto, Sydney, Paris, Frankfurt: Pergamon Press, 1980), pp. 4-5.

34. Simon, p. 328. Also see A. Doak Barnett and Francois Godement, "Science and the Struggle Between Two Lines," in Science and Technology in the People's Republic of China, Organization for Economic Cooperation and Development (Paris: OECD, 1977), pp. 204-216.

35. For example see Suttmeir, pp. 316-325.

36. Jimm Mann, "China Radically Alters Economy," Los Angeles Times, 21 October 1984, pp. 1, 14-15; and a preliminary report on China's increased willingness to boost fixed assets investment by Mark Baker, "China Plans Boost to Capital Investment in Energy Transport," Financial Times, 17 August 1984, p. 4.

37. See Gillespie, pp. 34-35.

38. Simon, pp. 307-312, offers a sophisticated assessment of this policy dilemma. For Japan's COCOM diplomacy, see William T. Tow, "U.S.-Japan Military Technology Transfers: Collaboration or Conflict?" Journal of Northeast Asian Studies 2 (December 1983): 14-18.

39. See Madelyn C. Ross, "Expert Controls: Where China Fits In," The China Business Review 11 (May-June 1984): 58-62; and David Shambaugh, "China's Defense Industries: Indigenous and Foreign Procurement," in Godwin, pp. 73-75.

40. "Concern Rises Over COCOM," China Trade Report 22 (September 1984): 12-13; and Paul Mann, "COCOM Agrees on Export of Computers," Aviation Week & Space Technology 121, 4 (23 July 1984): 21-22.

41. These points are analyzed in depth by Leonard Sullivan, Jr., with Ellen L. Frost and David S. Holland, "Trade and Technology Transfers," in China: Policy for the Next Decade, pp. 297-315.

42. See the remarks of Malaysian Prime Minister Mahathir bin Mohammed to visiting U.S. Secretary of State George P. Shultz as reported by Bernard Gwertzman, "Shultz Warned by Malaysia on Supporting China Growth," International Herald Tribune, 10 July 1984, p. 1.

43. For the latest Soviet comments on this matter consult David Buchan, "Soviet Warning Over U.S. Sales to China," Financial Times, 2 July 1984, p. 8.

44. As quoted in "Softer Line on Hardware," China Trade Report 21 (July 1983): 8.

3

Implications of the Post-Mao Reforms on the Chinese Defense Industries

Richard J. Latham

Zhang Jingyi, one of China's important civilian strategic analysts, observed recently that China was a Third World state which had to face "certain superpower problems."[1] According to Zhang, those problems were primarily of a national security nature. In studying these issues, Zhang noted that Chinese policymakers and analysts have focused on international factors. Domestic considerations, such as party politics, budgetary constraints, and emerging research and development capabilities, were much less frequently analyzed. Thus, in Zhang's estimation the defense posture and strategy of the People's Republic of China (PRC) have mainly reflected policymakers' rational responses to various threats posed by foreign states. It was in this context that Zhang proposed that over the last thirty years China's "basic defense strategy" had not changed in spite of profound domestic political turmoil.

Zhang's statements are provocative for several reasons. First, they suggest a continuity in strategic thought that Western analysts may be tempted to dismiss given China's domestic record of significant policy shifts. Second, his remarks run counter to our (American) experience in which domestic issues have strongly influenced the determination of defense strategy.[2]

The purpose of this chapter is to challenge the view that various aspects of China's national security policy can be understood primarily in terms of international, systemic influences. To the contrary, this chapter argues that any analysis of basic defense strategy must include a consideration of domestic budgetary issues, economic policy debates, emerging research and development capabilities, and defense industrial capabilities.[3] This is certainly not a novel approach in most defense policy studies, but according to Zhang, students of Chinese defense policy should not place much emphasis on domestic factors.

Zhang's suggestion that China's "basic defense strategy" has not changed is essentially correct. A similar case can be made that the defense strategy of the United States has not changed fundamentally since the early 1950s. That does not mean, however, that there have not been important shifts. Indeed, what has attracted our analytical attention have been the shifts which have taken place at the margins and have thereby allowed us to claim that the basic strategy has not changed.[4] In the case of China, there has not been a radical or announced policy shift away from "People's War" to large-scale nuclear deterrence, but there have been important, largely incremental changes which have taken China toward something we might call "modernized people's warfare."[5]

It is in this light that the question is addressed: To what extent might China's recent domestic economic policies and reforms affect national security policies and programs? Of necessity, the following analysis is speculative, but it should underscore the realization that the domestic reforms, which began with the Chinese Communist Party's (CCP) Third Plenum of the Eleventh Party Congress in December 1978, represent more than mere organizational adjustments which are unrelated to national security questions. The post-Mao economic, organizational, and democratic reforms have had and will continue to have a significant impact on Chinese national security matters.

THE POST-MAO REFORMS

The reformist impulses in China are similar to those found in most socialist states.[6] The targets of the reforms have included the following:

-- the economy (e.g., planning, efficiency, price structures, taxation, economic levers, commodity production, distribution networks, and employment strategies).

-- the bureaucracy (e.g., organizational reform, personnel recruitment, technical expertise, "unhealthy" bureaucratic practices, and decentralization of decisionmaking).

-- democratic procedures (e.g., rule by law, representation in the workplace and in government agencies, and relaxation of cultural, educational, and social controls).

-- internal party affairs (e.g., restrictions on the party's involvement in production and management, procedural reforms, greater democratic representation, and changes in the role of "political and ideological work").

-- foreign affairs (e.g., "open door" policies, trade, negotiation of international loans, greater involvement in non-communist international organizations and activities, increased scientific and technological imports, and tourism).[7]

This chapter's objective is not to document the nature and breadth of China's reforms. That is a task which is still underway.[8] It will be helpful, however, to note briefly how extensive these reforms have been. The point is that the reforms have involved more than token adjustments in policy and bureaucratic organizations.

Agriculture

The introduction of the household production responsibility system (ban gan dao hu) has resulted in abandoning large-scale collective agriculture. Communal organizations have been retained only as economic rather than administrative units, while townships (xiang) have been restored and charged with administrative responsibilities. Production responsibility has devolved to individuals, households, and specialized groups. The ethic of "daring to become rich" prevails and has eclipsed many of the egalitarian ("iron rice bowl") Maoist values. Consequently, the cornerstone of Mao's rural economic programs has been radically altered.[9]

Organizational Reforms

In breaking the "iron rice bowl," reformists also have sought to eliminate non-productive, redundant personnel and lighten the personnel overhead costs of production units. This has occurred at all levels from the central ministries to local production teams. A search for younger, leading cadres has also led to a widespread personnel upheaval. While the tenacity and cleverness of the entrenched party and civilian bureaucrats cannot be underestimated, the evidence of cadres' frustration and resistance suggests that the reforms have represented more than rhetorical eyewash.[10]

Democratic Reforms

The tendency in the West is to view with suspicion any official Chinese assertion that democratic reforms are being successfully advanced. This is especially true when we consider the "retrenchment" that followed the eventful days of Democracy Wall.[11] Recent Amnesty International charges of political intolerance in China also have contributed to our scepticism.[12] Without intending to appear excessively naive, we must acknowledge, however, that across a broad spectrum China has become more open and increasingly tolerant of both external and internal diversities. A pluralism of sorts has developed. The term "liberalization" has sometimes been used, but that concept, which we have largely borrowed from Soviet and East European reform scholarship, has been eschewed by the official Chinese press and party leaders.[13]

Economic Reforms

In general, economic reforms have touched sensitive issues and problems for orthodox communist cadres. These have included debates about centralized versus decentralized planning, the use and abuse of incentives, the appropriate economic roles for banks and investment loans, the use of economic levers in managing the "supplementary role of the market mechanism," the appropriateness of the concept of socialist profits, the relative priority of consumerism and investment, and the possibility of deregulating some aspects of the traditionally sacrosanct central control of pricing. Even now, seven years into China's reforms, there has not been a throughgoing termination of programs or discontinuance of discussions of these issues.[14]

Industrial Economic Reform

The proposed reforms in industry have been every bit as thoroughgoing as in agriculture. In practice, however, it has proven easier to decentralize rice production than industrial manufacturing. Consequently, industrial reform has moved more haltingly. Despite efforts to decentralize planning, the communist party and central planners still retain a decided interest in controlling prices, investment policies, capital construction, and the distribution of key resources. The central planners have tried to be less intrusive by ostensibly relying on the use of economic levers (e.g., taxation, profit retention schemes, banking and loans, and incentive programs), but their skills and knowledge have been as unevenly successful as one finds in capitalist states.[15]

CONTRADICTORY REFORM THEMES

The post-Mao reform movement has resulted in several general themes which have not always been compatible or consistent. These themes have involved the "Four Modernizations" (agriculture, industry, science and technology, and defense), "socialist material civilization," "socialist spritual civilization," production responsibility systems, "daring to become rich," economic efficiency, profitability, and consumerism (commodity production). The funding for the Four Modernizations has involved trade-offs and deferred investment or equipment acquisition. "Socialist material civilization" and "socialist spiritual civilization" are billed as being complementary, but actually they are often at odds with each other.[16] "Daring to be rich"--popular as it is--also has given rise to so-called ultra-individualism, economic anarchy, and a decline in collective values.[17] Economic efficiency has been advocated, but matters of equity and egalitarianism have been displaced. The emphasis on profitability has threatened the positions of central planners and local managers whose bureaucratic domains face closure or consolidation due to ineffective leadership, poor quality control, or "irrational" supply and marketing systems.[18] And finally, the emphasis on consumerism has been in conflict with the investment strategies of central planners.

NATIONAL SECURITY PLANNING: THE SIMPLE GLOBAL MODEL

Zhang Jingyi confirmed that the Chinese government does have a regularized national security policy and planning process. Unfortunately, he provided no explanation as to how defense planners translate threat perceptions into strategy and a resulting affordable force structure.[19] If we use Zhang's approach to analyzing Chinese defense strategy, we might arrive at the brief, linear relationship shown in Figure 3.1.

FIGURE 3.1

The Relationship of the International Environment
to Defense Strategy and Force Structure

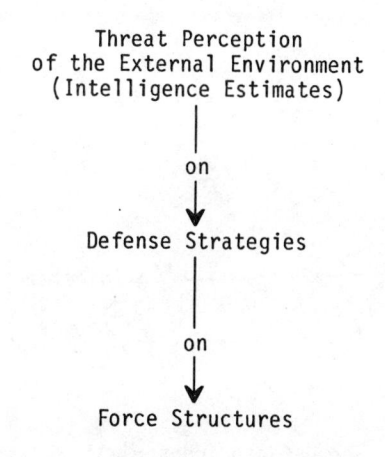

Threat Perception
of the External Environment
(Intelligence Estimates)
|
on
↓
Defense Strategies
|
on
↓
Force Structures

This model is useful as far as it goes. It suggests, however, a degree of rational reaction to threats that almost never exists in the real world. Threat perceptions invariably are subject to bureaucratic and political manipulation or questioning; planners and political leaders adjust strategies--albeit at the margins--to counter the threats; and desired force structures are trimmed to affordable levels usually as a result of domestic economic and political pressures.

NATIONAL SECURITY PLANNING: GLOBAL AND DOMESTIC LINKAGE MODEL

We are in need, therefore, of a more complex model that takes into consideration domestic political and economic factors. A tentative model is shown in Figure 3.2.

FIGURE 3.2

National Security Planning and Strategy:
  Domestic and Global Relationships

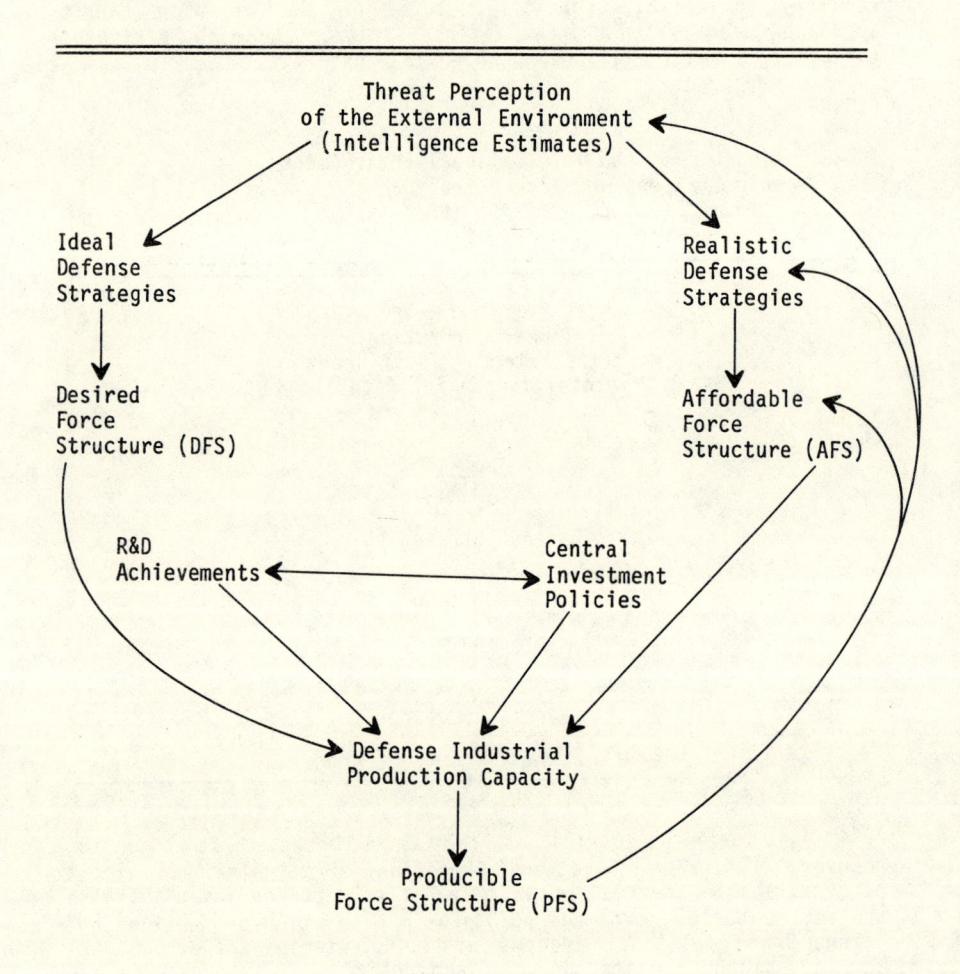

```
                    Threat Perception
              of the External Environment ◄─────┐
                 (Intelligence Estimates)        │
                  ↙              ↘               │
        Ideal                      Realistic     │
        Defense                    Defense  ◄──┐ │
        Strategies                 Strategies  │ │
           ↓                          ↓        │ │
        Desired                    Affordable  │ │
        Force                      Force    ◄──┤ │
        Structure (DFS)            Structure (AFS)
            │                         ↑        │ │
            │   R&D           Central │        │ │
            │   Achievements ← Investment      │ │
            │      ↘         ↙ Policies        │ │
            │        ↘     ↙    ↓              │ │
            └──→ Defense Industrial ◄──────────┘ │
                 Production Capacity             │
                         ↓                       │
                    Producible                   │
                    Force Structure (PFS) ───────┘

                                         Feedback
```

National security strategies, force structures, and--in centrally planned economies--defense industrial investment and production should be closely linked to threat perceptions and analysis. Concurrently, emerging defense research and development achievements should stimulate the consideration of possible strategic refinements, adjustments, or shifts in the force structure and new production technologies. The "producible force structure" (PFS) also should ideally be the same as the "affordable force structure" (AFS), and it should realistically address the threat. We are tempted to assume, incorrect as it seems, that in communist more than in market economy states, defense planners find it easier to establish a close "fit" between policy and force structure. Industrialized Western countries usually make only a distinction between the desired and affordable force structures. National security risk is sometimes measured by the disparity between the two structures (i.e., security risk = PFS - AFS). It is useful to make a distinction between a producible and an affordable force structure for China. The reason for this is that despite large investments in defense industrialization and research and development facilities, which have resulted in a comparatively large production capacity and research base, the producible force structure appears to have fallen short of the affordable force structure. Since the early 1980s, reform-minded economists have alluded to the defense industries as having a "golden rice bowl."[20] The metaphor has implied that the defense industrial system has been the recipient of large budgetary allocations without being subject to serious questioning about the need for or use of such funds. Following the CCP's Third Plenum of December 1978, critics began to note the contradiction between generous funding and an embarrassing underutilization of defense industrial facilities.[21] For the Chinese, then, the measurement of risk has become, in part, a function of industrial problems, not simply affordability.

In China, as in the industrialized West, there no doubt is a feedback loop between the ill-defined notion of risk and strategy. That is to say, strategy--notwithstanding the objective threat which drives force planners toward a particular force structure--can be politically changed to compensate for bothersome indications of risk which result from budget, technological, or production shortfalls.

Once again, the point is not to provide a fully developed picture of the development of national security policy in China, but to suggest that domestic economic policies and politics must be considered in any assessment of externally directed national security policy.

DEFENSE INDUSTRIAL IMPLICATIONS OF POST-MAO REFORMS

The logic of Figure 3.2 underscores several important points. First, there are qualitative and quantitative differences between PFS and AFS. To a certain extent, those differences will be a function of budgetary decisions, domestic budget priorities, and party politics. Second, the basic People's War strategy is determined as much by an affordable force structure as by external threats. Third, the acquisition of an affordable force structure implies at least a reasonable "fit" of force structure, strategy, and the enemy's threat. Finally, the bottom half of Figure 3.2 suggests that apart from budgetary politics, Chinese defense calculations must consider the "fit" between a producible force structure and the affordable force structure. The thrust of much of the criticism leveled at China's defense industrial system since 1980 is that there is a considerable difference between the force structure that government planners believed they were buying and the producible force structure that the defense industries were able to provide. There have been several long-term as well as recent reasons for this disparity.

First, Mao's notion of People's War has been a realistic but also an inhibitive strategy. On the one hand, it was a realistic reflection of and strategic approach for coping with external threats in the face of economic and military weaknesses. On the other hand, it also has been a damper on the emergence of industrially applicable defense-related research and development. Mao ostensibly approved of the development of modern military forces, but researchers, industrial leaders, and military officers always had bureaucratic if not political difficulty reconciling the requisite costs and force structures which were required to support two different strategies (e.g., modern or pre-war deterrence, and People's War or war-fighting capability).

Second, the Chinese government invested heavily in defense-related research and development. In the main, however, the investment does not appear to have developed <u>new defense technologies</u> that could influence strategic options and affordable or producible force structures as visibly or directly as Chinese officials would have liked.

Third, it appears that centrally planned capital construction in the defense industrial system was far in excess of what threat analysis, research and development capabilities, strategic thinking, and force structure dictated. Admittedly, this assertion is arguable. However, its basis is found in the fact that during much of the last thirty years, capital investment in heavy industry was particularly high. Consequently, in some areas of the Chinese economy there is now excessive industrial capacity while there are critical shortfalls in other areas (for example, in transportation and energy). The mere mention of "national defense requirements" was enough, however, to ensure a high priority for investment in defense industrialization and minimal objections from competitors for the scarce resources.

The recent domestic emphasis on economic efficiency, enterprise profitability, and consumerism has had a decided effect on China's defense industrial system. Since the mid-1950s China has invested heavily in a <u>segregated defense industrial system</u>. The history and organization of that establishment has been documented elsewhere.[22] What was not fully understood by Western observers was the extent to which that well-funded and comparatively modern sector of the economy contributed only minimally to the civilian sector.

Beginning in 1979, the quest for general economic reform drew unfavorable attention to the protected and inefficient defense industries. It appears, moreover, that when the reformists' principles of efficiency and profitability were applied to the defense industries, they were not accepted with much alacrity by the defense industrial managers.[23]

At the present time China faces a peculiar situation. On the one hand, it is seeking to import modern weapons systems from the West because its investments in defense research and development have not paid off. On the other hand, earlier, extensive investments in a defense industrial base, which has not been able to meet either the desired or affordable force structure that is dictated by foreign threats, leaves China with substantialy under-utilized defense production facilities. Chinese policymakers, therefore, are not facing new choices between defense and social welfare investments; rather, these investments in defense capitalization have already been made. The questions now are what is to be done with the excess production capacity, and how is foreign technology to be integrated with the domestic research and production capabilities.

The new domestic principles of economic efficiency, enterprise profitability, and consumerism have affected substantial shifts in the focus of the defense industrial establishment.

Economic Efficiency

For thirty years the defense industrial ministries have had first claim on human and material resources, and recent criticisms in Chinese journals suggest that the investments were subject to little or no cost accounting. Today, economic reformists are insisting that all sectors of the economy should be expected to demonstrate high levels of efficiency and effective utilization of resources. Across the board the quest for efficiency has posed quandaries for which there are no quick-fix solutions. For example, inefficient enterprises are expected to trim their staffs, but this policy conflicts with the pressing goal of providing full employment. Consistently inefficient plants in general are to be closed or consolidated. Civilian factories are particularly vulnerable, but defense industrial plants can and, no doubt, have claimed that cutting the "muscle"--or fat--of the defense industries is not prudent. Transferring scientific and technical personnel to non-defense industrial facilities is resisted because their skills are not necessarily required. The transfers also represent losses of occupational prestige and status for technicians.

Enterprise Profitability

The notion of profitability is now discussed extensively in

Chinese economic journals.[24] It is problematic, however, because profitability is linked to the price system. Tampering with the price mechanism has always been a thorny issue for socialist economic planners. Chinese economists now also write about a "supplementary reliance on the market mechanism." It is working to some extent in the area of consumer goods. The production of armaments poses entirely different problems. How do state defense industrial ministries set prices and exact profits from the state's sole domestic consumer--the Ministry of National Defense (MND)? In terms of armaments, however, it is a buyer's market in socialist states. The MND presumably determines its desired or affordable force structure based on its threat assessments. The defense industries, in turn, endeavor to meet the force structure demands. The relationship of the buyer and seller of defense equipment is so organizationally interrelated in China that one wonders to what extent the supplementary market mechanism can have any effect on profitability.

Consumerism

The solution appears, in part, to have been to direct the defense industrial ministries to use their excess resources and production capacity to manufacture civilian consumer products. In the official Chinese press, provincial and municipal National Defense Industries Offices have taken great pains to publicize how their subordinate enterprises, institutes, and schools have responded to the "domestic" demand for products and services.[25]

At first brush it appears that the defense industrial managers are solving the issue of profitable production of armaments by offsetting their production costs (losses) through the profitable sale of civilian consumer products and services. In the case of China the recent reforms have actually resulted in an anomaly in the armaments production of a so-called Third World country. Defense industrial facilities are being "retooled" for use in the civilian sector. Two goals are being met. First, a highly inefficient defense industrial sector is cutting or minimizing its losses. Second, pent up consumer demands are being partially satisfied by a heretofore pampered, technologically "advanced" sector of the economy.

PROBLEMS AND FURTHER ALTERNATIVES

From the standpoint of a Chinese economist or domestic policymaker, the greater integration of the defense industries into the general economy no doubt has been applauded. Defense planners, however, may hold a quite different view. Whereas a more efficient and profitable use of resources is presumably being realized, the defense planners almost certainly are asking whether or not the reforms have made it more possible to produce the desired or affordable force structure. Will the emphasis on consumerism result in an even less useful producible force structure?

The present domestic pressures for an efficient economy may have three serious consequences for China's defense system. First, defense industrial managers may have difficulty determining which master to serve. If the central authorities concurrently demand profitability (consumer goods) and defense production, socialist industrial leaders may face some difficult choices. In the near-term such conflicts should not be pronounced. In the long-run, however, if enterprise managers and management committees become accustomed to civilian market demands, they may find ways to delay, defer, or avoid meeting less profitable defense requirements.

Second, the perceived notion that traditional defense research, development, and industrial sectors have been over-funded in the past may result in at least a near-term under-funding of the defense industrial base. The result could be that the defense industrial system becomes even less capable of producing an affordable force structure. In other words, past excesses may lead to deferred investment.

Third, the re-channeling of some of the defense production capacity to consumer manufacturing may also result in deferred defense acquisitions.[26] The underlying logic is that in principle only the excess production capacity will be devoted to manufacturing civilian consumer goods. Presumably, therefore, the factories will then operate at near capacity levels. In reality, it is far more likely that the factories will continue to experience varying degrees of inefficiency, and part of the civilian production capability will be diverted from existing military assembly lines. Deferred acquisition eventually may result in logistic shortfalls and sustainability problems. The necessary costs and time to convert military factories back to full-time military production--if necessary--could be extensive.

One option which the Chinese clearly have adopted has not been discussed: participating in the international commercialization of arms transfers. One way to offset costly military imports and minimize the "civilianization" of its defense industries is to become an active participant in the growing sale of arms to Third World countries. In some respects, foreign observers have been slow to acknowledge this. On the one hand, observers have implicitly presumed that China would link arms sales to foreign policy objectives. On the other hand, it also has been assumed that China could not be a serious competitor in the international arms transfer market.

What became readily apparent in October 1984 at the Defendory International Exhibit at the Athenian port of Piraeus was that the Chinese fully intended to compete in the area of "low-tech" arms sales. Xia Wenxiang, deputy president of China's Academy of Electronic Technology, noted that "We're looking for exports. All our products are for sale with no strings attached." China, he said, expects to sell weapons "to Third World countries who are seeking reliable defense systems at budget-conscious prices."[27] One might say that the Chinese hope to become the K-Mart of conventional weapons sales.

NOTES

1. The views presented in this paper are those of the author and are not necessarily those of the U.S. Air Force Academy, the Department of the Air Force, or components of the Department of Defense. Interview with Zhang Jingyi, USAF Academy, Colorado Springs, Colorado, 27 September 1984.

2. See Amos A. Jordan and William J. Taylor, American National Security: Policy and Process (Balitmore, MD: The Johns Hopkins University Press, 1984); Robert P. Haffa, "Rational Methods, Prudent Choices: A Primer on Planning US Military Forces," chapter 3 of a manuscript to be published by the National Defense University Press, 1985; William W. Kaufmann, Planning Conventional Forces: 1950-80 (Washington, DC: The Brookings Institution, 1982).

3. Douglas J. Murray and Paul R. Viotti, eds., The Defense Policies of Nations (Baltimore, MD: The Johns Hopkins University Press, 1982), pp. 4-7. Also see William R. Heaton, Jr., "The Defense Policy of the People's Republic of China," in Murray and Viotti, pp. 419-440. Heaton does not explicitly address the implications of domestic determinants, although he does examine the decisionmaking process and civil-military relations.

4. See Richard Smoke, "The Evolution of American Defense Policy," in American Defense Policy, ed. John F. Reichart and Steven R. Sturn (Baltimore, MD: The Johns Hopkins University Press, 1982), pp. 94-135; and Jordan and Taylor, pp. 58-80.

5. Harlan W. Jencks, "'People's War under Modern Conditions': Wishful Thinking, National Suicide, or Effective Deterrent?" China Quarterly 98 (June 1984): 305-319.

6. See Richard J. Latham, "Comprehensive Socialist Reform: The Case of China's Third Plenum Reforms, Ph.D. Dissertation, University of Washington, Seattle, Washington, 1984. Chapters two and three specifically deal with the political phenomenon of "socialist reform."

7. A similar delineation of the post-Mao reforms is found in Harry Harding, "Reform in China: A Mid-Course Assessment," Journal of Northeast Asian Studies 3:2 (Summer 1984): 3-25.

8. See Stuart R. Schram, "'Economics in Command?' Ideology and Policy since the Third Plenum, 1978-84," China Quarterly 99 (September 1984): 417-461; and Noriyuki Tokuda, "The Socialist System under Transformation in Post-Mao China: Uncertain Explorations Toward Integration," Journal of Northeast Asian Studies 3:1 (Spring 1984): 17-29.

9. For a summary of the initial Western assessments of China's agricultural and rural economic reforms see Greg O'Leary and Andrew Watson, "Current Trends in China's Agricultural Strategy: A Survey of Communes in Hebei and Shandong," *Australian Journal of Chinese Affairs* 8 (1982): 1-34; Andrew G. Walder, "Worker Participation in Enterprise Mangement: The Complex Past of the Evolving Present," *Contemporary China* 3 (Fall 1979): 76-88; Wolfgang Kasper, "Note on the Sichuan Experiment," *Australian Journal of Chinese Affairs* 7 (1982): 163-172; and Audrey Donnithorne, "Prolonged Readjustment: Zhao Ziyang on Current Economic Policy," *Australian Journal of Chinese Affairs* 8 (1982): 111-126.

10. See Peter R. Moody, Jr., "Political Liberalization in China: A Struggle Between Two Lines," *Pacific Affairs* 57:1 (Spring 1984): 26-44; Parris Chang, "The Last Stand of Deng's Revolution," *Journal of Northeast Asian Studies* 1:2 (June 1982): 3-19; and David Zweig, "Opposition to Change in Rural China," *Asian Survey* 23 (July 1983): 879-900. Moody describes cadre opposition to the reforms in terms of the "red opposition" versus the "expert opposition" (pp. 26-27). Chang sees cadre opposition to the reforms as a function of ideological and factional loyalties. Zweig, on the other hand, see cadre opposition stemming from frustrations that result from losses of power, income and prestige.

11. Moody, p. 42.

12. *China: Violations of Human Rights* (London: Amnesty International Publications, 1984).

13. Moody, pp. 26-44; and H. Gordon Skilling, "Interest Groups and Communist Politics Revisited," *World Politics* 36:1 (October 1983): 1-27.

14. Lo Ping, "Another Major Victory for the Reformists," *Cheng Ming (Contending)* 85 (1 November 1984): 6-9, in Foreign Broadcast Information Service, *Daily Report: People's Republic of China*, 6 November 1984, pp. W-4; hereafter cited as *FBIS*.

15. See Yang Jisheng, "Theories, Blueprints, Experiments and Conditions--Investigation and Research on the Problems of Reforming the Economic Structure," *Jingji Yanjiu (Economic Research)* (hereafter cited as *JJYJ*) No. 4 (20 April 1982): 18-25, Xue Muqiao, "Problems to the Solved in Reforming the Economic Management System," *JJYJ* 1 (20 January 1982): 3-7, in *FBIS*, 24 February 1982, pp. K-11 - K-17; Zeng Guoxiang, "Macro Control and Regulation over Micro Economic Reform," *JJYJ* No. 7 (July 1982): 21-26; and Xue Muqiao, "Planned Economy and Regulation by Market Mechanism," *Shijie Jingji Dabao* (Shanghai), No. 89 (21 June 1982): 2, in *FBIS*, 14 July 1982, p. K-2.

16. Schram, p. 445. A thorough discussion of the conflict between "socialist material civilization" and "socialist spiritual civilization" can be found in Latham, pp. 465-512.

17. Zweig, pp. 879-900; and Huang Qiuyan, "The National Defense Industry Should Take the Road of Integrating the Military and Civilian Sectors," Jingji Quanli (Economic Management) (hereafter cited as JJQL) No. 7 (15 July 1981): 36.

18. Wang Guomin and Jiang Xiaoli, "An Important Way of Developing the National Economy--An Investigation of the Integration of Military Production with Civilian Production in the Course of Comprehensive Restructuring the Economic System in Chongqing City," Sichuan Daxue Xuebao (Journal of Sichuan University) No. 2 (April 1984): 9-12, in China Report: Economic Affairs (Arlington, VA: Joint Publications Research Service), 19 October 1984, No. 86, p. 42, hereafter cited as JPRS-CEA.

19. Zhang Jingyi interview, 27 September 1984.

20. Huang Qiuyan, p. 36.

21. Wang Guomin and Jiang Xiaoli, p. 42.

22. See Harlan W. Jencks, From Muskets to Missiles (Boulder, CO: Westview Press, 1982), pp. 189-221; Richard J. Latham, "People's Republic of China: The Restructuring of Defense Industrial Policies," in James E. Katz, ed., Arms Production in Developing Countries (Lexington, MA: Lexington Books, 1984), pp. 103-122; and David Shambaugh, "Military Modernization and the Politics of Technology Transfer," Contemporary China 3 (Fall 1979): 3-13.

23. Huang, p. 36.

24. See Gu Zongcheng and Sun Guanglin, "A Preliminary Study of the Characteristics of the Assumption of Sole Responsibility for Profits and Losses by the Enterprises under the Socialist Ownership by the Whole People," JJQL No. 7 (15 July 1981): 42-45, in JPRS-CEA No. 78978 (15 September 1981): 7-15; "Is the Motive Force of Economic Reform to Regard 'Money as Everything'?" Renmin Ribao (People's Daily), 27 June 1983, p. 1; and Yang Jisheng, p. K-5.

25. For example, see Ni Zhifu, "Create More and Better Forms of Army-People Cooperation," Jingji Ribao (Economic Daily) (Beijing), 31 December 1984, p. 3, in FBIS, 11 January 1985, p. K-20. See also: FBIS, 3 November 1980, p. L-22; 3 June 1983, p. R-10; 6 June 1983, p. R-3; 20 June 1983, p. R-3; and 10 August 1984, p. R-1.

26. Wang Guomin and Jiang Xiaoli, pp. 42-46. A number of articles cited declining demand for military products from 1979 to 1982. See Zhang Rumou, "On Military Industrial Enterprises

Following the Road of Military-Civilian Integration," <u>JJGL</u> No. 8 (5 August 1983): 6-8, in <u>JPRS-CEA</u>, No. 84556 (17 October 1983), pp. 88-89; and Chen Jiagui and Wang Lingling, "Exploit the Advantages of Military Industrial Enterprises to Serve Technical Transformations in Civilian Industry--An Investigation into the Wangjiang Machine Factory's Moves Toward 'Military-Civilian Integration,'" <u>JJGL</u> No. 8 (5 August 1983): 8-12, in <u>JPRS-CEA</u>, No. 84556 (17 October 1983), p. 82.

27. <u>Gazette Telegraph</u> (Colorado Springs, CO), AP dispatch, 17 October 1984, p. A11. See also: "Birth of an Arms Salesman," <u>The Economist</u> (London), No. 7368 (17 November 1984), pp. 40, 45.

4

Foreign Technology and Chinese Modernization[1]

Wendy Frieman

INTRODUCTION

A number of fundamental ambiguities and inconsistencies have characterized official U.S. policy toward China since 1979, when President Carter announced normalization of bilateral relations. Chief among these is the U.S. attitude toward China's military modernization. Beginning in 1980, U.S. and Chinese defense officials have repeatedly discussed the possibility of formal bilateral security cooperation, including such activities as coproduction of weapons, sales of defense hardware, and exchange of military personnel. Such cooperation would have been unthinkable ten years earlier. At the same time, U.S. policymakers seem to fear the possibility of military applications of foreign technology sold to China for ostensibly civilian objectives. As a result, high technology sales are routinely delayed for anywhere from six weeks to two years. Thus the signals have been mixed and it remains unclear whether the United States wants to encourage, participate in selectively, or prevent China's military modernization.

One factor contributing to the inconsistency in official U.S. policy towards China is the absence of a solid quantitative and analytical baseline understanding of China's military and technological capabilities. Assessments range from a sigh over the inability of China's industries, both military and civilian, to compete in the world marketplace, to a cringe at the prospect of a military giant on the Asian mainland. Neither of these positions, nor any intermediate position, is well supported by the kind of comprehensive, multi-source data available about the Soviet Union.

Thus, it is difficult to answer the following salient questions raised in conjunction with possible arms sales to China. First, exactly what do or will the Chinese want to buy? What kinds of systems? How many? How sophisticated? With what financial resources? Under what transfer arrangements? Second, how efficiently will the Chinese People's Liberation Army (PLA) use, deploy, or assimilate the foreign defense equipment and technology it acquires?

These broad issues require substantial elaboration before they can be answered with any certainty. What China wants to buy will be affected by, among other factors, who wants to sell and under what terms, by lessons learned in previous wars, by changing threat perception, and by the state of the current inventory. How effectively technology will be assimilated, in turn, depends on the organizations involved in the transfer process, the degree to which defense factories in China are able to implement Western management techniques applicable to high-tech industries, the procedures used to transfer both hardware and knowledge, and the capabilities of the recipient factories and research institutes. None of these second-level issues has been thoroughly addressed by either the scholarly China community or the defense policy community.

The purpose of this chapter is not to provide the definitive answers. Rather, it focuses on those questions about the role of foreign technology in China's military industries that can be addressed with some confidence. Despite imperfect data, it is possible to talk about certain issues: How has China developed weapon systems in the past? What role has foreign technology played and for what reasons? What transfer mechanisms have been important or effective? To what extent are current strengths and weaknesses in the defense industries attributable to the use of foreign expertise or technology during earlier periods? Is history a guide to what may happen in the future? What is the Chinese leadership currently doing to upgrade the PLA's weapons? How does foreign technology fit into the current program? Is the current strategy likely to succeed?

Before making conclusions concerning the history of technology transfer and current and future Chinese policy, it is helpful to examine the different means that China has used to acquire weapons since 1949.

MECHANISMS FOR WEAPON PROCUREMENT IN POST-1949 CHINA

The framework that follows is the result of a system-by-system examination of what is believed to be currently in China's weapons inventory, how each weapon was acquired or manufactured, and what kinds of foreign assistance were involved. Historical and technical data have been collected on over 100 Chinese systems, although evidence of foreign involvement in many of them was scarce or non-existent and had to be inferred from secondary works. The sources examined were primarily defense reference works such as Jane's, but monographs and articles in technical journals that discuss China's defense capabilities were also reviewed.[2] From this technical and historical data it appears that China has used six major mechanisms to acquire weapons. These are listed, along with the weapons they were used to acquire, in Table 4.1. It should be remembered that the data about Chinese weapons tend to be anecdotal and incomplete, making it extremely difficult to assign individual systems to any one category with a high degree of certainty.

Table 4.1

China's Mechanisms for Weapons Procurement-Pre-1985

Indigenous R&D and Production	Produced with Soviet Assistance Prototypes	Reverse Engineered	Modifications of Chinese or Foreign Equipment	Recent Coproduction Agreements
CSS-1 MRBM Medium-Range Ballistic Missile	J-5 Fighter	Q-5 Fighter/Bomber	2-9 Turboshaft Helicopters	U.S. M18-A1 Rifle
CSS-2 IRBM Intermediate-Range Ballistic Missile	H-5 Bomber			German 7.92 mm Maxim Machine Gun
CSS-3 Intercontinental Ballistic Missile	Z-5 General-Purpose Helicopter	Mi-8 General Purpose Helicopter	Pratt & Whitney Aircraft Engines	Soviet Single 85 mm Dual-Purpose Gun Mounting
CSS-X-4 Intercontinental Ballistic Missile	Z-6 General-Purpose Helicopter	Type 63 107 mm Multiple Rocket Launcher	Spey Aircraft Engines	
107 mm Type 63 Multiple Rocket Launcher	130 mm Gun Mounting	SA-2 Guideline Missile	Float Glass Technology	Japanese Kamishima-class Escort
CSX-NX-3 Submarine-Launched Ballistic Missile	100 mm Dual-Purpose Gun Mounting	Atoll Air-to-Air Missile		British Guangzhov-class Escort
Xia-class Submarine	37 mm Antiaircraft Gun Mounting	Type 36 57 mm Recoilless Rifle		Australian Luo Yang-class Escort
Han-class Submarine	Type 62 Light Amphibious Tank	Type 59 Main Battle Tank		
Luda-class Destroyer	Type 63 Light Tank	Type 69 Main Battle Tank		U.S. 1-511 LSTs (now used as tankers)
Type 24 Machine Gun	Type 55 Armored Personnel Carrier	Type 531 Armored Personnel Carrier		
Type 26 Machine Gun	Golf-class Submarine	90 mm Anti-Tank Rocket Launcher		
	Romeo-class Patrol Ship	90 mm Anti-Tank Rocket Launcher		
	Anshan-class Destroyer	Haikov-class Fast Attack Craft		
	Cross Legs, Thick-skin, Chop Rest Early Warning Radar	Kronshtadt-class Large Patrol Craft		

Indigenous R&D and Production

China has designed and produced a number of weapons with minimal foreign assistance. The ICBM, IRBM, and satellite programs are perhaps the best examples. China tested its first atomic bomb in 1964 and its first megaton-range thermonuclear weapon in 1967, making the transition from a fission to a fusion weapon in three years. The Second Artillery, believed to be the nuclear missile arm of the PLA, now deploys four ICBMs with a range of 7,000 kilometers and an impact of 103 megatons, in addition to several ICBMs with a range of roughly 13,000 kilometers and an impact of between five and ten megatons. The MRBM/IRBM force consists of approximately 135 missiles with ranges of 1,800 to 2,500 kilometers. All these missiles are liquid-fueled, and foreign defense analysts have questioned their vulnerability and accuracy. A solid-fueled, land-based missile is probably under development but has not been tested. A solid-fueled SLBM was tested successfully in 1982.

It is worthwhile noting here that the Chinese did not undertake a nuclear program with the intent of "going it alone." Mao Zedong held high hopes in 1956 that the Soviets would transfer nuclear weapons technology, which they finally refused to do three years later. Chinese disappointment over this decision contributed to the mounting tension in Sino-Soviet relations. Mao later expressed gratitude to Khrushchev for forcing China to develop its nuclear program completely independent of Soviet involvement.[3]

In addition to the nuclear program, China has launched fifteen experimental satellites since 1970, having mastered the technology necessary for deceleration, reentry, and landing. These accomplishments suggest that the PRC is developing the capability to launch manned spacecraft. Finally, it is noteworthy that China has independently designed and produced two nuclear-powered submarines after exposure to Soviet Romeo- and Golf-class models. The first Han-class submarine, of which there are now approximately six, was tested in 1974 and was used in naval exercises in 1980 and 1981. The Xia-class submarine, first tested in 1981, was used for an April 1982 test of China's CSS-NX-3 ballistic missile.

These are impressive achievements for a nation struggling to achieve comprehensive modernization and faced with massive demands on limited financial and manpower resources. Although these systems may not be comparable to the latest generation U.S. or Soviet weapons, they form an important component of China's deterrent which has been demonstrably successful in preventing large-scale attack or invasion from foreign powers. Moreover, they indicate that China has the capability to carry out independently the research, development, design, and production of weapons that involve a range of sophisticated technologies from ballistics to electronic guidance and control.

A central question remains why certain areas, such as nuclear science, have been so successful, whereas others have been considerably less impressive. The evidence suggests that the nuclear program has enjoyed certain privileges denied other military projects; however, very little is known about exactly how either the nuclear or conventional weapons-related R&D effort has been organized and managed in China. Recently data have begun to emerge, mostly in the form of autobiographical writings or discussions with Chinese scientists, that may shed some light on this issue.

Coproduction with the USSR

A second mechanism for weapons development in China was close cooperation with Soviet scientists, engineers, and technicians. China received broad-ranging economic and technical assistance from the Soviet Union in the 1950s under an arrangement that has been referred to as the largest technology transfer experiment in history. Assistance in weapons production was only one component in a much larger trade and aid program that included the delivery of equipment and raw materials, long- and short-term credits, and Soviet participation in the construction of over 200 large capital projects for civilian as well as military industries. In conjunction with this package, the USSR sent literally thousands (estimates are around 10,000) of advisors to work in and manage Chinese factories and institutes, and, in 1958 alone, Soviet educational institutions accepted over 12,000 Chinese students and "trainees." Prior to 1949 China did not have the basic industries required to raise the standard of living and build a modern defense, namely steel, petroleum, machine building, and electronics. The Soviets simply moved in and built these industries in China virtually from scratch.[4]

It is difficult to document the role that military assistance played in total aid, but it is likely that it amounted to at least half the financial value of the package. Many questions can be raised about the appropriateness of the Soviet model to China's economy, or about the long-term effects of such massive assistance, but the arrangement inarguably gave the Chinese a weapons-producing capability that would have required significantly more time to develop indigenously. The Soviets provided the PLA with prototypes, blueprints, and in some cases, entire production lines for virtually every category of conventional weapon, including fighters, bombers, infantry weapons, armored fighting vehicles, military radar, surface-to-air and surface-to-surface missiles, and military communications systems. The Chinese were ultimately able to mass-produce many of these systems independently even though the Soviets withdrew their assistance abruptly for ideological reasons in 1960. In this respect, the transfer experience must be considered at least a partial success.

The costs of earlier over-dependence on Soviet equipment and expertise, however, become painfully clear to the Chinese in the early 1960s. Although Chinese engineers had been well trained, they had not acquired the capacity to perform the basic R&D

functions required to manufacture new systems independently. It is still unknown whether this was because the Soviets genuinely did not want China to have such a capacity, or because there simply had not been adequate time to educate a generation of Chinese scientists and engineers in complex and demanding disciplines. Whatever the reason, the skills of the technical workers did not compensate for the weak links in the defense production chain, namely concept formulation, design, and systems integration and management. The result is that the PLA has been mass-producing obsolete weapons for the past fifteen to twenty years. The Chinese are now keenly aware of how earlier overdependence on the Soviet Union contributed to their current difficulties, but it is difficult to identify a "quick fix" solution. Once again, the nuclear and satellite programs remain exceptions, as these are areas where the Chinese have designed new systems and made the transition from R&D to production entirely on their own.

Reverse Engineering

A third method China has used to acquire weapons is reverse engineering. Over the years the PLA has obtained prototypes for a large number of foreign systems and then dissected them to learn how to duplicate the systems. Reverse engineering was, in fact, the chief mechanism for weapon procurement between 1960, when Soviet aid was withdrawn, and the early 1980s.

Among the weapons the PLA has reverse engineered is the J-6 fighter, also often referred to as the F-6. This aircraft is a Chinese version of the Soviet MiG-19, which was planned for coproduction with the Chinese in the 1950s. When Soviet advisors left China in 1960, the production lines for this aircraft were incomplete. Nevertheless, China was able to manufacture over 100 J-6s by 1964 and to modify the aircraft extensively, the modified version appearing around 1970 as the Q-5 (also referred to in Western writings as the F6bis, the F-9, and the A-5). The Chinese J-6 appears to be comparable in all respects, including speed and fire control systems, to the Soviet MiG-19, and there are reportedly close to 2,000 of them still in service.

Unfortunately, by the time China had managed to correct some serious start-up problems and begin serial production, more advanced combat aircraft capable of faster speeds were entering the forces of other countries. Thus the fighter that now constitutes the backbone of China's air force has been obsolete for over ten years. For this system, the actual process of reverse engineering appears to have ultimately been successful, but the time required to make it work gave other contries the opportunity to supersede the earlier design, and left China well behind the technological curve.

A second example of reverse engineering in China's armed forces is the production of the SA-1 Guideline surface-to-air missile. This, too, was a planned coproduction project with the Soviets. China has manufactured and deployed a few hundred

Guideline missiles despite the untimely withdrawal of Soviet blueprints and assistance. This missile is reportedly for use against medium-altitude targets and is primarily useful for forcing down enemy aircraft to a point where they are in the range of China's (Soviet-supplied) antiaircraft guns. The Chinese-manufactured systems were reportedly effective against U.S. jets in Vietnam, although Soviet advances in electronic countermeasures since the war may diminish the usefulness of this missile in a conflict with the Soviet Union. The Chinese also copied the <u>Atoll</u> air-to-air missile which is, in turn, a Soviet copy of the U.S. "Sidewinder" infrared homing air-to-air missile. <u>Atolls</u> are deployed on China's J-4 and J-6 fighters. Very little is known about the performance of the Chinese version as compared to its U.S. or Soviet counterparts. At best, it is now ten years out of date, and there is no evidence of later generations of either the <u>Atoll</u> or the "Sidewinder" in China today.

In summary, the Chinese have been able to reproduce foreign systems, in some cases without blueprints or technical advice, to achieve the technical and performance specifications of the prototypes. The most notable successes have been in aircraft, machine guns, naval gun mountings, submarines, and tactical missiles. The central problem in China's reverse engineering effort concerns the resources that were required for the effort and the degree to which the success of these projects affected the next generation of weapons. For all the reverse-engineered systems described above, the cost in time was critical. While the Chinese were perfecting production methods and raw material processing techniques for 1950s generation weapons, the technological world moved ahead. Advances elsewhere, particularly in the United States and Soviet Union, quickly made the Chinese systems obsolete. The Chinese were especially hard hit by significant advances in electronics technology that did not become incorporated into and are not accounted for in most Chinese aircraft and armored fighting vehicles. Furthermore, it seems that once a large-scale reverse engineering effort such as the J-6 was successful, it became a mainstay of China's weapons inventory. Scarce resources that had been expended on the project were not then immediately available to invest in a more advanced system.

Ultimately reverse engineering could not compensate for the design capability that China's defense factories lacked, and were unable to acquire from copying foreign prototypes, however successful individual transfers may have been. The problems inherent in a strategy of relying solely on reverse engineering have been amply discussed by Hans Heymann in his study of China's aircraft industry:

> Every major design feature of a complex, modern piece of equipment is the outcome of a large number of engineering compromises and tradeoffs, the results of stress calculations, laboratory experiments, and functional tests. 'Understanding' the design to the point that the copier can ultimately improve upon it means knowing <u>why</u>

the compromises were made and how these tradeoffs were arrived at. The copier cannot learn this from studying the finished prototype.[5]

Modifications to Chinese or Foreign Systems

A fourth method used by China for developing defense hardware, the modification of existing systems, is also a function of the PLA's weakness in system design and integration. When Chinese engineers could not design new weapons, they improvised with the weapons they had. Virtually every Chinese weapon has been tinkered with by PLA engineers who appear extraordinarily adept at making marginal modifications on systems that have been in serial production for some time.

The Q-5 fighter, referred to briefly above in conjunction with the J-6, is an example of such a modified system. The Q-5 project began in the mid-1960s, the Chinese well aware by then that the maximum speed of the J-6 (Mach-1.75) would be inadequate in most combat situations. By 1970, PLA factories were able to begin serial production of a fighter capable of Mach-2 speeds that outperformed the J-6 in a number of other important respects as well. Its fuselage was 25% longer, its fuel tank was substantially larger, and its engine is believed to be more reliable, requiring less service and enabling more flight hours before replacement. The PLA Air Force now deploys approximately 200 of these planes.

Another example in this category is the Twin 57-mm antiaircraft gun mounting. This is an upgraded Chinese version of the Soviet S1F-31B model gun to which the PLA has added a lead-computing optical sight for fire control, thereby substantially improving its accuracy. Finally, although this short list is by no means exhaustive, many of China's fast attack craft have been modified to allow for a steel hull, a refined mast, and more sophisticated weapons. Other types of systems that the Chinese have been adept at modifying include machine guns and armored personnel carriers.

In each of the instances described above, as well as many others, the PLA has been able to make a virtue of necessity. Lacking the design talent required to develop an entirely new generation of weapons, weapons factories have been able to modify existing systems in such a way as to measurably improve their performance or survivability. It is difficult to find evidence of how these weapons have fared in combat, but what data exist suggest that the workmanship is of extremely high quality. It should be remembered, however, that modifications of foreign prototypes were sometimes intended not to improve performance, but to "Sinify" the system. This is most likely the case for many of China's infantry weapons which differ from foreign models only in cosmetic features.

Coproduction With Other Countries

A fifth method used by China's defense industries can be loosely termed "arm's length" coproduction. The open-door policy of the early 1980s and subsequent liberalization of the economy have made it possible for foreign firms to participate in upgrading China's military factories. Nevertheless, the cooperation is not as close as that between the Soviet Union and China in the 1950s.

The most well-known of the arm's length coproduction agreements is that between Rolls Royce of the United Kingdom and the Chinese Ministry of Aeronautics Industry to manufacture Spey engines at an engine factory in Xian. This assistance package was rather broad in the range of services provided despite the fact that it was limited to the technology for one specific aircraft engine, and included provisions for training upwards of 700 Chinese personnel. It also provided for transfers of material, equipment, processes, and technology. British managerial and technical experts worked side by side with their Chinese counterparts at the factory in Xian. Yet after three years the Chinese were still unable to mass produce the engines on their own; the six engines that were manufactured to British specifications had all been handcrafted.

Another recent coproduction agreement was signed in 1980 between China and Aerospatiale of France to produce fifty <u>Dauphin-2</u> twin-turboshaft helicopters. The first was test-flown successfully in 1982. This helicopter is to be used initially to support offshore oil rig operations, but it could also be used in any number of combat scenarios. Very little information is available about how well this coproduction arrangement has been working since 1982; at that time there was speculation that the test flight was of a helicopter produced, in fact, entirely by French personnel, albeit on Chinese soil.

Recent coproduction arrangements differ from the earlier Soviet experience in a number of important respects. These represent isolated projects rather than pieces of an integrated, comprehensive aid package. This has occurred in part because Chinese planners have sought to avoid overdependence on any one source of material, equipment, or expertise. This approach also reflects the belief of China's leadership that China should not look to any one foreign economic, scientific, or military system as the model for China to emulate. Instead Chinese planners appear to be choosing individual systems, technologies, and methods, and to be seeking to incorporate them into a distinctive Chinese model of development.

It is too early to tell how quickly or efficiently the PLA will be able to modernize its entire inventory through this kind of piecemeal approach. Neither of the two projects described above appears to have been an overwhelming success. Nevertheless, it may be a mistake to evaluate solely the output of these ventures and ignore the lessons of the experience and the scope of China's learning curve. History is unlikely to repeat itself exactly, and the next transfer of aircraft engine techology may well proceed much more quickly with more impressive results. Furthermore, reforms in the Chinese economy and improvements in the scientific and technical infrastructure, discussed briefly below, are beginning to affect operations in military factories and are likely to contribute to a more receptive climate for future transfers.

Captured Systems

Finally, it is worth mentioning that China still has a number of foreign-manufactured systems in its inventory, primarily naval escorts and infantry weapons. Many of these were captured during combat, some as long ago as 1948-1949. The parade by Communist troops into Beijing on October 1, 1949, is said to have been the most extensive public display of U.S. military hardware in over a decade. China also has captured Australian, German, Czech, and Japanese weapons. Although these systems are by and large obsolete by world standards, they have helped to fill gaps in PLA capabilities when the military lacked the resources to develop or acquire modern weaponry. Some may have provided prototypes of reverse-engineering projects.

SUMMARY OBSERVATIONS ON THE HISTORICAL PERSPECTIVE

Five general conclusions can be drawn from the PRC's experience with these mechanisms. First, foreign equipment, material, technology, or advice has been not an incidental, but a critical feature of conventional weapons production in China since 1949. The PLA received some kind of foreign assistance in manufacturing virtually every category of conventional weapon, as well as military support equipment such as helicopters, trucks, radio sets, radars, and so forth.

Second, the form of this assistance has varied considerably over time, ranging from the large-scale "hands-on" involvement of the Soviet Union to the occasional use of U.S. systems captured from the Nationalists by the PLA in the 1940s. Thus the PLA has been somewhat flexible in its approach to acquiring and assimilating foreign weapons technology. To be sure, this flexibility may often have been born of necessity; the deficiencies of the PLA have been severe and in many cases there have been few alternatives from which to choose when it came to foreign assistance.

Third, PLA engineers have been quite adept at independently reproducing and modifying the foreign systems they have acquired, and now have the capability to manufacture an impressive array of conventional as well as strategic weapons. Foreign observers have commended the Chinese on the quality of the workmanship evident in Chinese-manufactured weapons that have been sold or given to other countries. The problem with the PLA's inventory appears to have more to do with the date of the designs and of the production equipment than the standard of workmanship.

Fourth, China's extensive use of foreign technology has had significant long-term costs for the defense modernization effort. The PLA's engineering talent has been consumed by the painstaking task of reverse engineering and modifying foreign weapons to such a degree that the military industrial complex has not been able to cultivate enough professionals capable either of creating new designs or incorporating major technological developments, such as those that have characterized the electronics industry, into weapon system production. The defense industries, furthermore, have not learned to manage the integration of large, complex systems effectively. This is due in part to China's lack of adequate computers, advanced instrumentation, automation, and CAD/CAM technology, and in part because the officials responsible for defense production do not have the necessary project management skills. It appears that all too often China has begun with the finished system and worked backwards, rather than beginning with R&D relevant to certain keystone technologies and building up from there.

Fifth and finally, different ministries, services, factories, and research institutes within China's military-industrial complex appear to have significantly different experiences in absorbing technology and, relatedly, different capacities for undertaking wholly indigenous R&D projects. The submarine, nuclear missile, and satellite programs all seem to constitute "pockets" of excellence, whereas aircraft engine design and military electronics have long been weak links in the defense production chain. It is easy here to run the risk of overgeneralizing based on uneven amounts of data--much more is known about the fighter program than, for example, about China's air defense weapons. Undoubtedly as more information about the development of different systems becomes available, more strengths and weaknesses will be evident.

These are at best tentative conclusions and represent little more than the starting point from which a range of additional questions emerge. One relatively unexplored issue is _why_ foreign technology has had such an influential role in the development of China's military industries. What alternatives might have been available? Has the decision to use foreign assistance been made for primarily military, political, ideological, or economic reasons? Have the reasons for looking to foreigners for assistance changed over time? How long would it have taken China's military factories to enjoy the same degree of success independently?

Another question that needs to be examined is the reasons for the success or failure of specific transfers. Exactly where did the Spey engine project founder? Did the problem lie in faulty material processing, poor quality control, inadequate technical personnel, inefficient management, insufficient allocation of capital to the project, overly optimistic expectations, or some other factor? Why were other transfers more successful? Did their success have more to do with the level of technology being transferred or with the efficacy of the transfer mechanism? How have changes within the Chinese military and economic system over the past twenty years affected the country's ability to assimilate foreign technology--in other words, would a Soviet-style transfer be as effective today as it was in the 1950s?

Finally, is history an accurate guide to the future? Will the long lead time required for reverse engineering and "learning-by-doing" through licensing preclude forever China's ability to design and manufacture independently, or can exposure to foreign technology be structured in such a way as to accelerate the process of military modernization? The answer is in large measure contingent on the success of policies now being promoted by the Chinese leadership, which are described in the following section.

CURRENT POLICIES FOR MODERNIZING CHINA'S WEAPONS INVENTORY

It is possible to at least suggest the future course of China's defense industries by examining current policies aimed at the modernization of PLA defense technology. Since 1979 the Chinese leadership has promulgated a number of integrated policies that constitute a coherent, deliberate strategy for improving the quality of weapons in the PLA inventory over the next five to ten years.

Finished Weapon System Purchases

Despite speculation in 1980 that the PLA was only window-shopping and had little intention of making any purchases abroad, China has begun to buy finished military equipment. Among the systems reportedly sold to China are a French long-range radar system and $140 million worth of U.S. helicopters. It is true that finished weapons sales are expensive, and that cost will place an upper limit on how much can be imported. In addition, political problems could arise in some supplier countries, among them the United States, if a very ambitious program of military assistance were undertaken. Nevertheless, it is at least possible, if not likely, that modest purchases, targeted at specific weaknesses, will continue as China's foreign exchange earnings grow.

Technology Transfer Agreements

China's leaders recognize that purchases of individual weapon systems will be at best a short-term band-aid approach to improving China's military capability. In military, as in civilian technology imports, the Chinese are less interested in purchasing the finished product than in acquiring the technology and expertise required to manufacture the equipment themselves.

It is for this reason that China is pursuing technology transfer agreements with U.S. and European firms to upgrade PLA weapons manufacturing equipment and processes. Discussions are underway for "substantial" coproduction agreements between the United States and China in anti-armor technology, and there has been mention of coproduction of a U.S. fighter aircraft in China.[6] Other transfers with direct military application include the agreements with Rolls Royce to coproduce Spey aircraft engines and the licensing of float glass technology from Pilkington Brothers (U.K.) for optical systems in military aircraft.[7] The PLA is also receiving assistance from Europe and Japan in casting technology that is needed for jet engine housings, aircraft wings, brakes, bearings, and turbine blades. It seems that similar agreements with major U.S. weapons manufacturers are being contemplated seriously by both sides.

Incremental Improvements to Existing Systems

Incremental improvements to current systems, using both foreign- and Chinese-developed technology, are evident in a number of new Chinese weapons. Electronic warfare is an area where small improvements can make important differences. The value of incremental change can be seen in the appearance of the T-69 main battle tank, which is an upgrade of the T-59 to incorporate an infrared searchlight and a laser range finder. With a relatively small capital investment, the PLA was able to alter substantially the performance characteristics of this main battle tank which, while not as effective as its Soviet counterpart, is of value in a number of scenarios. Advances in electronics may well translate into performance improvements for many outdated systems, especially fighter aircraft, destroyers, and armored fighting vehicles. It is also likely that the PLA will make other incremental modifications, such as improving ammunition quality and gun stabilization.

Improving the Technical Sophistication of Defense Personnel

China's leaders are keenly aware of the role that trained technical personnel must play in the development of modern weapons systems. The current leadership has instituted a series of military reforms designed to increase the supply of trained professionals, and to strengthen the S&T infrastructure within the services. This policy is consistent with, and reinforced by, the drive throughout China to foster scientific and engineering talent. S&T requirements are now built directly into the PLA's recruiting and education process. College graduates in technical fields are being aggressively recruited, while senior officials with inadequate technical skills are being retired.

The PLA is also implementing S&T education programs for all soldiers, regardless of rank, as well as for workers in defense factories who may not necessarily be part of the formal military structure. One of the mechanisms for training PLA personnel is establishing regional training bases with the backing of local universities and colleges. Cadres who need advanced knowledge in specialized areas are released from production duties to attend classes for three to six months at a time. Conferences and meetings to exchange papers on military science and personnel are being reported frequently in the press; lectures, films, and foreign S&T journals are now available as part of a "continuing education" effort for PLA personnel. Finally, overseas training for officials from defense factories and research institutes will probably also play some role in this effort, although to date it has been difficult to document what fields are being pursued in foreign universities and how effectively these individuals are being used when they return to China.

Acquisition of Foreign Civilian Technology

Much of what is gained through the successful absorption of foreign civilian technology can ultimately benefit the military sector. This is no doubt one reason for the keen interest Chinese aviation industry officials have displayed in links with U.S. aircraft firms. The potential for military application of civilian technology is also evident in China's purchases of sensing and detecting technology. Sophisticated seismic equipment purchased for offshore oil exploration can easily find applications in undersea sensors, instrumentation, and navigation systems for submarines. Infrared detectors, gyrocompasses, surface acoustic wave devices, and conventional and laser gyroscopes can find application in military guidance and control systems.

China is also interested in acquiring microwave technology, specifically amplifiers, switches, modulators, and passive components such as antennae, filters, and duplexes which can find military application in radar, electronic warfare receivers and jammers, and fire control. China has been quite aggressive in acquiring a range of foreign electronics technology and systems, specifically computers and peripherals, many of which can ultimately support military purposes. Integrated circuits and memories associated with mainframe and mini-computers are also crucial to military command, control, communications, and intelligence capabilities.

Finally, purchases of satellites and additional ground stations are likely to add to China's image processing and reconnaissance capability. It is, in fact, because of potential military applications that the sale of the Landsat ground station has been held up for several years by the U.S. government pending the resolution of policy differences on exporting advanced technology to China.

Not surprisingly, the very things the PLA most wants (sophisticated manufacturing technology, blueprints, designs, and processes) in these important "dual use" sectors are the items that supplier nations find it most politically troubling to supply. The U.S. government, for example, has been much more forthcoming in its offers to sell China advanced tactical weapons than in its offers to help China solve underlying infrastructure problems associated with weapons production.

Promotion of Key Civilian Sectors

China's sixth five-year plan calls for accelerated growth in a number of sectors directly and indirectly related to weapons production, among them automotive technology, shipbuilding, and electronics. This means that these industries will have access to the scarce resources required for rapid modernization: skilled manpower, budget allocations, foreign exchange for technology purchases, quotas of students to be sent overseas for training, and capital equipment. The China State Shipbuilding Corporation, the China Automotive Industry Corporation, and the Ministry of Electronics Industry all produce military as well as civilian goods, and if the current rhetoric, which calls for more communication and coordination across bureaucratic lines, is translated into practice, it is almost certain that some civilian advances will spill over into the military arena.

THE FUTURE OF CHINA'S DEFENSE INDUSTRIES

The policies enumerated above bear some similarity to the historical mechanisms described earlier in this chapter; however, a number of differences suggest that the outcome may be substantially different from that of past efforts to acquire modern defense technology. It appears that China will not be caught forever in a technological time trap, always having to copy acquired weapons one step ahead of indigenous capabilities. First, China's leaders appear to have reasonable expectations about foreign technology and defense modernization. Chinese articles on military modernization no longer gloss over hardware deficiencies in favor of lengthy treatises on People's War, a strategy that downplays the role of modern weaponry. Nor is acquisition of modern technology for the military sector seen as a panacea for everything that ails the PLA. Thus the program is likely to enjoy modest success and continued political support.

Second, it appears that the Chinese leadership now has a more sanguine understanding of the weak points in the military establishment than was evident in earlier periods. Events that have occurred between 1978 and 1984, such as the coproduction agreement with Rolls Royce and the war with Vietnam, have provided opportunities to reevaluate military capabilities and objectives and fine-tune long-term strategies for defense modernization. Thus resources can be effectively targeted against the areas of greatest need. Current policies appear both practical and workable within the Chinese context.

A third major difference is that today Chinese leaders are on a two-track program to both import advanced technology to overcome specific problems in the short term and develop a first-rate indigenous military R&D and production capability over the longer term. Acquisition of foreign technology is only one of a number of mechanisms, and there is a growing emphasis today on activities that will strengthen China's indigenous S&T base so that it will be able to support a vigorous defense R&D program in later years.

Although in earlier periods lip service was paid to technical self-sufficiency, today those works are backed up by pragmatic policies at all levels of the military-industrial system.

Zhang Aiping, appointed as Minister of National Defense in 1982, rose through the ranks of China's defense S&T system and has stressed the relationship of modern technology to national defense. In a major article in <u>Red Flag</u> in 1983 he stated:

> In order to achieve modernization of our national defense, our first task is to develop and produce sophisticated military equipment. This work demands the comprehensive application of all modern science and technology and involves very complicated systems engineering. Moreover, in the process of developing and producing the equipment, we should also have a series of means to experiment and test equipment, and many kinds of new materials and technology. Solution to these problems involves the basic involvement of science and technology--including all its fields such as basic theory, technological science and, to a very great extent, applied technology and engineering technology. We can say that any progress made in this work closely depends on modern science and technology and that without these we can never make any progress or achieve anything in this work...It was in 1958 that we began to develop our country's strategic nuclear weapons. From the very beginning, (veteran PLA leader and CCP member) Nie Rongzhen insisted that the broad ranks of scientific and technical personnel should know not only "how" but "why." Therefore we organized the scientific and technological forces of our national defense scientific and technological units, the Academy of Science, industrial departments and higher education institutions and forces of all our provinces, municipalities and autonomous regions to divide up their tasks and cooperate with one another...[8]

Another recent article in the Chinese journal <u>Systems Engineering--Theory and Practice</u> reported on a conversation with Qian Xuesen, a key scientist in China's nuclear missile program, who underscored this point: "How exactly should we equip our country's army? We should fully utilize modern science and technology, encouraging the strong and avoiding weak points.... In order to build a modern army, we must also have comprehensive knowledge of military science and technology."[9]

Finally, the current program also differs in that it involves a conscious decision to blur the distinction between civilian and military production. China's leaders expect that advances in the civilian economy will ultimately benefit military programs; for this reason they are undertaking a number of structural reforms designed to ensure succcessful communication and cooperation in dual-use sectors. The merging of ministries to form integrated civil-military companies is only one example of these reforms.

Much work remains to be done on these issues. The access to Chinese aircraft and electronics research and factories that U.S. scholars and corporate representatives have begun to enjoy can provide the opportunity to fill some of the gaps in our knowledge about China's defense industries. There is a need to know more, for example, about how defense factories have been managed. There is also a need to know about the extent to which policies affecting civilian industries, specially the decentralization of authority and the "responsibility system," are affecting military factories and institutes.[10]

Another key issue to examine is how China goes about determining specific priorities for procuring foreign military technology. The requirements of the PLA are vast, the lead times long, and the resources finite. What determines individual acquisitions? Is it strategy, threat perception, current capability, interest group politics, availability on the world market, price, foreign policy, or some combination of these factors?

An equally important question relates to how Chinese leaders view their own experience. What lessons have they learned, above and beyond the dangers of overdependence on a single supplier, that will affect their acquisition of foreign systems in the future? What transfer mechanism do the Chinese themselves see as being most desirable or efficient? It is hoped that future research will address these questions.

In conclusion, the current policies and programs for modernizing Chinese defense technologies do not entail unsupportable expenditures; all appear both practical and possible. Foreign technology is seen as a catalyst that will promote technological change from within. If the policies outlined above are implemented consistently over the next five years, foreign observers will see a substantial improvement in both China's ability to assimilate foreign technology and capacity to develop and produce modern weaponry indigenously. Whereas any one of these policies looked at singly may appear to have little effect on overall capability, if policy continuity is maintained, together these activities may well be found to equal more than the sum of the parts.

NOTES

1. This chapter is an excerpt from a longer study on weapons acquisition in China that I wrote with the generous support of SRI International. I am grateful to Denis Simon, Tom Fingar, and Harry Harding for their comments on various drafts of that paper. However, any errors or inaccuracies must be considered my own.

2. See, among other sources: <u>Jane's All the World's Aircraft, 1983-1984</u> (London: Jane's Publishing Co., 1983), pp. 33-41; <u>Jane's All the World's Aircraft, 1970-1971</u> (London: Jane's

Publishing Co., 1971), p. 19; Jane's Armour and Artillery, 1982-1983 (London: Jane's Publishing Co., 1982), pp. 2, 252, 553, 614, 661, 761, 895; Jane's Fighting Ships, 1983-1984 (Jane's Publishing Co., 1983), pp. 99-107; Jane's Infantry Weapons, 1978 (London: Jane's Publishing Co., 1978); Jane's Weapon Systems, 1983-1984 (London: Jane's Publishing Co., 1983), pp. 19, 73, 77, 249, 376, 415; Jane's Weapon Systems, 1973-1974 (London: Jane's Publishing Co., 1973), p. 62; Harlan Jencks, From Muskets to Missiles (Boulder, CO: Westview Press, 1983), pp. 156, 198; William Kennedy, "The Defense of China's Homeland," in Ray Bonds, ed., The Chinese War Machine (London: Salamander Books, 1979), p. 76; Hugh Lyn, "China's Navy--for Coastal Defense Only," in Ray Bonds, ed., The Chinese War Machine (London: Salamander Books, 1979), p. 175; Harvey Nelsen, The Chinese Military System, 2nd ed. (Boulder, CO: Westview Press, 1983), pp. 164, 232; David Shambaugh, "China's Defense Industries," in Paul Godwin, ed., The Chinese Defense Establishment (Boulder, CO: Westview Press, 1983), p. 56, 57; and Bill Sweetman, "The Modernization of China's Air Force," in Ray Bonds, ed., The Chinese War Machine (London: Salamander Books, 1979), pp. 134, 137, 139.

3. "Story of A-Bomb Told by Program Chief," New York Times, 5 May 1985, p. 15.

4. Jacques Guillermaz, The Chinese Communist Party in Power (Boulder, CO: Westview Press, 1976), pp. 82-83.

5. Hans Heymann, China's Approach to Technology Acquisition: Part III. Summary Observations (Arlington, VA: Rand Corporation, 1975), p. 30.

6. "U.S. Eyes Assistance to China of F-8 Fighter Program," Aerospace Daily, 24 July 1984, p. 121.

7. "Major Licensing Agreements Since 1975," Business China, 15 September 1982, p. 133.

8. "Zhang Aiping Writes on Defense Modernization," in FBIS Daily Report: China, 17 March 1983, pp. K3-4. Originally published in Chinese in Hongqi, 5 (1 March 1983): 1.

9. "Qian Xuesen on Military Science Technology," JPRS China Report: Political, Military and Sociological Affairs, 29 September 1983, pp. 92-93. Originally published in Chinese in Systems Engineering-Theory and Practice, 2 (1983): 1.

10. See Robert M. Field, "Changes in Chinese Industry Since 1978," in China Quarterly 100 (Dec. 1984): 741-761, for a discussion of these reforms.

5

Chinese Weapons Development: Process, Progress, Program?

John Frankenstein

Two approaches serve to illuminate the issue of Chinese weapon systems development. The first views weapon systems development as a decision process, while the second sees it as a problem in the application of innovation--in other words, as a technology transfer issue. We begin with the decision process, looking for inputs to outputs for the black box of Chinese decisionmaking and substituting "threat" for input and "military response" for output. (Subsets of the latter term would include weapon systems, military organization, and military doctrine.) Thus even if there is little explicit knowledge of the decisionmaking process itself--which, indeed, is the case--items that are considered in or produced by that process can be identified and specified.

The model requires some assumptions which should be identified. First, if we assume that the goal is Chinese military security, then we also assume that decisions about the response are needs-driven--that is, some assessment of the threat enters into the decisionmaking process. At the same time we should recognize that both short-and long-term considerations enter into the process. Immediate security needs drive the short-term process, but long-term development objectives--essentially, the establishment of China as a great power in the international system--also play an important role.

Approaching weapon systems development from the technology transfer/innovation perspective allows additional insights. If Chinese military decisions can be considered to be needs-driven, and the needs are perceived as changing, then the process can be looked upon as a change, or innovation, process. Additionally, it is apparent that the process is subject to the same considerations, the same strengths and weaknesses, as other sectors of the Chinese technologies world. Accordingly, we can apply existing knowledge of other aspects of Chinese technology and technological decisionmaking to the problem.

A technology transfer/innovation approach also permits focusing on yet another set of variables. These would include: organizational issues; industrial resources; design issues; management questions; barriers to innovation; and cultural influences.

In short, these approaches and assumptions permit transforming a poorly understood process into a problem which, while hardly simple, is at least manageable. The first approach draws attention to external factors; the second to internal concerns. It may be that the subject has been over-systemized: some observers are of the impression that, in Richard Latham's words, "even informed (Chinese) officials do not think in terms of a formal, conceptualized acquisition process."[1] Although the details of Chinese military decisionmaking are unknown, some indications of how the Chinese view their international and military situation are known, as well as data on how the Chinese have deployed and equipped their forces. Additionally, the larger issues confronting the Chinese with respect to innovation and technology acquisition are identifiable.

EXTERNAL FACTORS: THE THREAT

Chinese statements concerning international politics have varied in detail over the past several years, but there is one constant--the Soviet threat. To be sure, the Chinese today condemn the "intense contention" between the superpowers. In his 1984 National Day address Deng Xiaoping spoke of "the seriously deteriorating international situation" and reiterated Chinese opposition to "all aggression and hegemonism"--code words for U.S. and Soviet policy actions.[2] But despite this rhetorically even-handed treatment, it is the "social imperialists" and "hegemonists" who clearly pose the immediate military threat.

A glance at the map will show, indeed, that key Chinese cities and industries are only a few hundred miles from the Soviet border. Shenyang, the industrial center of Manchuria and the site of major aircraft, tank, and ordnance work, lies just under 500 miles from Vladivostok.

The precise military nature of the Soviet threat is, however, deserving of a closer look. Some observers claim that about one-third of all Soviet forces are in the Far East. The U.S. Department of Defense includes fifty-two army divisions (450,000 troops), 1,820 tactical aircraft, eighty <u>Backfire</u> bombers, two aircraft carriers, 126 submarines, eighty-eight major surface combatants, and 120 SS-20 IRBMs in its accounting of the current Soviet order of battle in Asia--total manpower estimates are in the 750,000 range. Furthermore, these forces have grown considerably in both quality and numbers. Since 1978, the total number of ground force divisions has increased by around twenty percent, and both surface combatants and tactical aircraft have grown about thirty percent.[3]

Without trying to deny that the Soviet buildup is substantial, it should be noted that neither are all of these forces targeted on China, nor are they all arrayed along the critical Chinese northeast border. The Soviet Union has other security concerns in the region, including Japan, the United States, and the Korean dilemma, not to forget their Vietnamese client. Also, not all of the Soviet ground divisions are at full strength--some analyses suggest that only seven or eight Soviet Army divisions along the border are at full Category I strength.[4] Nonetheless, this could represent a combat-ready force of around 100,000 troops and over 2,100 tanks.

The Chinese Responses

How have the Chinese responded? First, a sizeable percentage of Chinese forces are in the north, deployed around critical cities and industries. According to the International Institute of Strategic Studies, eight of China's thirteen armored divisions (62%) are stationed in the North or Northeast Military Regions; forty-four or 37%, of the PLA main force ground divisions and twenty-six, or 36%, of local force divisions are deployed in the same regions; this does not include several border troop divisions.[5] Assuming deployment at full strength, Chinese main combat forces in the north number around 664,000 troops and 5,440 tanks.

Thus in sheer numbers alone, Chinese ground forces in the North and Northeast are approximately equivalent to the entire Soviet Far East deployment. Furthermore, in combat-ready manpower, it would appear that China has roughly a five to one advantage. The question is, of course, whether bodies are sufficient--the conventional wisdom is that China needs to upgrade on all levels--air defense, anti-armor, and so on. It would seem that at best China has struck a defensive position of minimal deterrence. So far, that has been enough.

But to achieve this, the Chinese Armed Forces have seen substantial growth. Based on data provided in the IISS annual, Military Balance, the total PLA manpower has grown by 40% over the past decade from about 3 million to 4.2 million; for the same period, ground force manpower grew over 50%, from 2.5 million to 3.9 million; air force manpower has been increased by over 120% from 220,000 to 490,000, and naval manpower from about 230,000 to 360,000, an increase of over 55%. Organization and equipment have likewise grown--IISS counted seven armored divisions in 1974, and thirteen in 1984, and the number of tanks organic to a main force infantry division went from thirty-two to eighty.[6] Total combat aircraft increased from 3,800 to 5,300; and the number of submarines and major surface combatants have both roughly doubled, from fifty-one to over one hundred and from seventeen to thirty-five respectively. Finally, in 1984 we should note that it appears the Chinese made their strategic rocket forces a separate branch; IISS estimates that China now has around 114 such weapons. To be sure, one should treat all these figures with some caution, but it is the relative trend, not the absolute figures, that is most revealing. (Figure 5.1 shows total PLA manpower growth from the mid-1960s and indicates a very rapid growth in the period 1974-1978.)

FIGURE 5.1

Manpower Growth in the Chinese Armed Forces, 1964-1980*

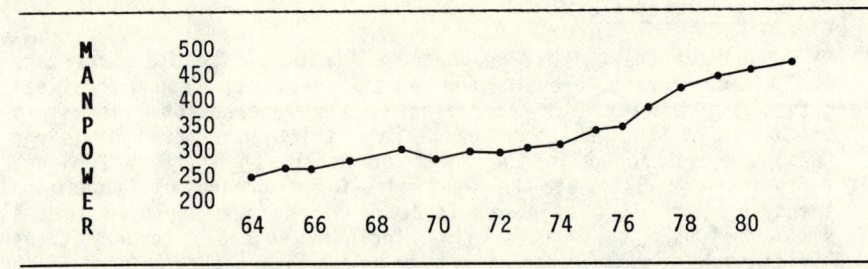

```
M         500
A         450
N         400
P         350
O         300
W         250
E         200
R             64   66   68   70   72   74   76   78   80
```

*Source: IISS <u>Military Balance</u>, various years.

Before we proceed further, we should acknowledge that force structure growth is not the only response the Chinese have mounted to what is clearly perceived as a threatening international environment. Rather, the Chinese have attempted to improve the quality as well as increase the quantity of their forces. More important in a larger global and historical context, China has emerged as a major actor in the international system. Since the early 1970s, Chinese diplomacy has been remarkably successful in establishing China's international trade.

Still the immediate military security issue will not go away. What are the international implications of the force structure growth sketched above?

INTERNAL CONCERNS: ORGANIZATIONAL ISSUES

First, it is important to recognize that this growth has occurred in a very poor country. This suggests that not only have military affairs enjoyed a high priority, but also, and perhaps more importantly, that the Chinese industrial system has been forced to meet that priority. Certainly one gets the impression from talking with knowledgeable Chinese that the army is seldom denied the resources it wants.

The core of that system is fundamentally Soviet, and was installed in the mid-1950s as part of the vast Soviet assistance program. At the same time, the Chinese military inventory was built up with Soviet weapons. The scope of this assistance was remarkable; as General Samuel Griffith has written, the Soviets "gave their Chinese allies the best they had available."[7] To be sure, much of this military assistance was related to the Korean War, but it did result in the thorough Sovietization of Chinese weapons designs. The combination of a Soviet inventory base and a Soviet industrial system has determined the course of weapon system development in China and, indeed, will continue to do so for some time to come.

Thus Chinese industry is built on the Soviet model in terms of both technology and organization. There are six military industrial ministries, all vertically organized on the Soviet model, which answer to the Chinese State Council, the Ministry of National Defense and various state commissions, including the State Science and Technology Commission (SSTC) and the Commission of Defense Science, Technology and Industry (CDSTI). Basic science is dominated by the central Academy of Sciences.[8]

This type of organization has been criticized for its bureaucratism, barriers to communication and innovation, and inherent inefficiencies. Studies of the Chinese bureaucracy give weight to twin issues of personalism on the one hand, and bureaucratic rigidity and "turf protection" on the other. The current season of economic reform is targeted on just such barriers. While the impact of the reforms on the military industries is unclear, there are some indications that many aspects apply, ranging from the use of the technical resources of military industries for civilian production to increased organizational freedom, profit retention, and relaxation of constraints on contracts. Thus the North China Industries Corporation, part of the Ordnance Ministry, is attempting to branch out into foreign sales and enter into deals with foreign firms. New corporations, such as Polytechnic, a dependency of the China International Trust and Investment Corporation but directed by officials with high-level PLA contacts, are also becoming involved. Interestingly enough, some military industrial organizations may have gone further than intended--in early 1985, for instance, the Fuzhou military industries were included in a general, economy-wide round of criticism directed at "unhealthy tendencies"--speculation, profiteering ("buying up and reselling at a profit materials and goods in short supply"), unauthorized price rises, and the creation of dummy companies.[9]

The Soviet Legacy

Given the Chinese industrial debt to the Soviet Union, it is useful to review what is known about the Soviet weapons development system. It has been characterized as being fundamentally conservative, with improvements and advances coming incrementally, rather than in blazing breakthroughs. As A. J. Alexander of RAND has suggested, this is as much a response of the system as it is a reflection of the state of Soviet science:

> The general tendency in Soviet weapons is for relatively simple designs, designs that make much use of common subsystems, components, parts and materials; that are evolutionary in their improvements; and that are comparatively limited in performance ... The inflexibility of centrally planned economies is an additional constraint on weapons R&D. Because of

>unreliability of supply and inability to rely on contracts or plans to guarantee deliveries, designers are reluctant to ask for new products ... They face strong incentives to use off-the-shelf components that can be counted on to perform to acceptable (though perhaps not optimal) standards.[10]

As a result, Alexander points out, the entire weapons development system in the USSR is "shaped by formal procedures," including a "unified system of design documentation" that is overseen and coordinated by the powerful Military-Industrial Commission (VPK) and the State Committee for Science and Technology.

If, as we have noted, procedures in China may not be as formal, the organization mode looks familiar, with the CDSTI fulfilling the role of the VPK. Similarly, as Hans Heymann has noted, the relationship between research and development (R&D) and design in the Chinese aircraft industry follows the Soviet model, with research institutes, separated from design and production functions, passing on the results of their research in design handbooks which describe in detail processes to be followed.[11]

None of this seems designed to strike intellectual sparks down the line, and it all finally lands on the shoulders of the factory chief engineer, who has to cope with not only technical, but economic, managerial, and political responsibilities as well. Studies of the civilian sector suggest that R&D plans from the top have difficulty penetrating down to the enterprise level, hampered by the isolation of R&D institutes from production and by a lack of funds for new ventures. Such innovation as there is tends to be fragmented, occurring at the enterprise or factory level, directed by the chief engineer.[12]

Industrial Manpower

From this brief description, it should be clear that successful innovation in such a system is highly dependent on the quality of personnel at the enterprise or factory level. Skilled manpower takes the longest of all national assets to develop and is one of China's most pressing problems. As PLAAF chief Zhang Tingfa noted in late 1984, "Knowledge and talented persons are essential to the development of production ... At present we are short of qualified people, and our scientific and technological foundation is weak."[13] This is only an echo of a constant theme heard throughout China today.

The rehabilitation, reform, and growth of China's S&T and educational systems in recent years are dramatic stories. But our concern here is to sketch the state of China's technical manpower. Estimates for the late 1970s suggested that there were approximately 1.2 million scientists and engineers of varying qualification in China. More recent Chinese figures have put the number of "scientists and technicians" in the 5.7-6.2 million range, with some 338,000 engaged in research; but only 10% of these are, as Denis Fred Simon puts it, "described as 'senior scientists', or scientists with advanced degrees and training equivalent to their counterparts in the West."[14] Indeed, this elite .5% of the Chinese scientific establishment may be senior in more than just academic qualification.

In sum, the key issue is quality, and here, by Chinese admission, the outlook is not bright, it would appear that the Chinese engineering talent pool is adequate to keep the factories producing at their current technical levels. There are questions about the next step.

Design Issues

When we turn to examine the weapon systems that are in the Chinese inventory, we see the results of the Soviet legacy. Not only are all major Chinese weapon systems based on Soviet designs, but they remain essentially at the level at which they were introduced. This is not to say that there have not been developments. Indeed, there have even been model number changes, but the change has been incremental, and attempts to make breakthroughs have not been successful. We can get an idea of how the weapons development system works by taking a brief look at the tanks and aircraft now deployed by the Army.

Tanks

Tanks and other armor, of course, represent a mature technology. The main Chinese battle tank, the Type 59, is based on the Soviet T-54, a 1950s design. The tank has been slowly upgraded with infra-red night vision gear and laser rangefinders; some have also been experimentally fitted with British passive night vision systems. The latest version, now called the Type 69-II, includes an up-grade main gun (from the original 100mm smooth bore to a British designed 105mm rifled gun), infra-red capability, gun stabilization, NBC protection, and an "automatic fire-control system."[15]

Chinese light tanks, the T-62 and T-63, also show the Soviet influence. Both carry an 85mm main gun, an adaptation of the Soviet D-44 anti-tank gun. The T-63, according to Jane's, is "virtually a scaled down Type 59 MBT"; the T-62 is based on the Soviet PT-76 light amphibious tank and retains its water-jet capabilities.[16]

It should be clear that the improvements and adaptations reflected here are essentially conservative. There are few if any indications that China has moved toward improved armor types or advanced munitions; indeed, according to one knowledgeable observer, it could be that China's most basic armor need is under the hood--Chinese tank engines operate with great difficulty, if at all, in the long deep freeze of a Manchurian winter.[17] The requirement for simply getting the product out the door appears to be a major factor; the number of armored divisions over the past twenty years has increased three-fold (from four to thirteen), which for armor alone suggests a growth from about 1,200 to 3,600 tanks. When we factor in the 119 main force infantry divisions, each with an organic tank battalion of from thirty-two to eighty tanks, plus the additional ninety-six tanks that are attached to each of the thirty-five Chinese armies, we can see that the army's full main battle tank complement numbers around 13,000.

Aircraft

When we turn to aircraft, we see the same process: incremental improvements on Soviet designs. And some of the Chinese difficulties with advanced military technology can also be seen in this sector.

Growth too has been an issue. Over the past two decades, the PLAAF combat aircraft inventory has increased by 130%, up to 5,300 airframes from 2,300, by IISS count. Most of these, (around 3,000), are J-6s, the Chinese version of the MiG-19. The plane has been in Chinese production since the late 1950s. In the late 1960s or early 1970s, the Chinese developed a fighter-bomber, the Q-5, based on the J-6 airframe and engines; this appears to be a substantial modification of the original design. About 300-400 are estimated to be in service today. Other Soviet-designed Chinese built aircraft flown by the Chinese include 120 H-6s, based on the Tu-16 <u>Badger</u> and 550 H-5s, the Chinese version of the Il-28 <u>Beagle</u>.

The outcomes of attempts to upgrade the fighter force are unclear in the open record, although the fact that the Chinese have been able to standardize on a fighter the Soviets could never quite refine is probably no small accomplishment. The Chinese attempted to manufacture the MiG-21 in the 1960s, only to run into production problems. While it was thought that production had ceased, the reported supply of MiG-21s to Iraq suggests that the production facilities for the aircraft have been reopened, if, indeed, they were ever shut down.[18]

And despite speculation about the sale of advanced Western fighters to the China--even in the early 1960s the Chinese were talking to the Swedes about the J-35B <u>Draken</u>[19] --the Chinese apparently have preferred to stick with what they know--Soviet designs. There are reports of Chinese experiments with MiG-23s acquired from Egypt, and a prototype J-8 was exhibited to U.S. officials in 1980. This aircraft, which looks like a stretched MiG-21 but which carries two engines, has not gone into serial production. It is not, apparently, a success; an experienced Western fighter pilot who has examined the aircraft rather directly termed it "a dog."[20]

It is understandable that the Chinese remain faithful to their Soviet engineering roots, especially when we see what happened when they tried to adopt relatively advanced Western engine technology. It is well known that China has a license from Rolls-Royce to produce the Spey engine, which powers British F-4 Phantoms. The precise status of this project remains unclear, but if even half of what is said unofficially about the Spey episode is accurate, the project does not appear to be a happy experience for all concerned. For example, it was reported that the engine simply would not fit into the airframe the Chinese had designed. Additionally, and perhaps more importantly, there were significant design, engineering, and manufacturing problems associated with the engine.

Simply put, the design principles used by Soviet and Western engineers to solve the problem of increasing jet thrust are different. Soviet designs, particularly those of the 1950s and 1960s on which the Chinese were raised, approach the problem through increased airflow and high fuel comsumption rates. Western designs, on the other hand, emphasize higher operating temperatures, and thus require hard-to-handle specialty metals and exotic materials. And it was in this area that the Chinese apparently ran into serious difficulties. From the time the license was obtained in late 1975 until at least late 1980, the Chinese had to make additional purchases of advanced machinery and equipment from the West to keep the project going. Although it is reported that four Chinese-assembled engines eventually did pass initial acceptance tests, the tone of these reports suggest that the project no longer has the high priority it once enjoyed.[21]

Current Technological Levels

In sum, in China we find a military-industrial complex producing thirty-year old designs. If we accept the paradigm that charts a nation's military-industrial development from simple maintenance through licensed assembly and parts production to, at least, indigenous original design and manufacture, China appears to be somewhere between the penultimate and final stages. This outcome is the result of a number of factors, including: a mode of technology acquisition through plant imports, licensing, and reverse engineering; a strategy which stresses reproduction, not design development; organizational rigidity; conservative engineering philosophies; and personnel/human capital shortfalls.

As we shall see below, the Chinese are aware of the need to "catch up." We need to turn next to the options which are open to them.

Imports

One solution to the Chinese modernization dilemma would be to turn to the international arms market. There are many convincing arguments for upgrading the weapons inventory by purchasing them from the West. The Chinese can pay for them--Chinese gold and foreign exchange reserves are now approximately $20 billion. Furthermore, Chinese forces have experience in dealing with a mixed weapons inventory. There is a demonstrable need for such weapons, and, indeed, the Chinese have made a few foreign weapons or "dual-use" deals, including arrangements for Bell helicopters, civilianized Sikorsky Blackhawks, and jeeps. Certainly the Chinese have stimulated a lot of interest in possible purchases.

Over the past decade they have examined or expressed interest in an astonishing array of military goods; Chinese military bureaucrats have engaged in extensive window shopping--and information collecting--tours through the West, most recently in the United States. What happens to the brochures, pictures, and manuals obtained from these trips is unknown; perhaps there is an office in the CDSTI in which they are filed. But we do know that the Chinese are relatively current on military developments: publicity photos of Hellfire ATMs, AH-64 Apache attack helicopters, cruise missiles and the like are displayed on the second floor of the Chinese Military History Museum in Beijing, and Jeifangjun Huabao (Liberation Army Pictorial) regularly runs features on modern military technology.

An examination of the weapon systems the Chinese have expressed an interest in sheds some light on their hardware modernization priorities. Most have to do either with aircraft or electronics, and the third priority concerns tactical defense. Nonetheless, few contracts for complete systems have been finalized. Indeed, in some areas, such as ATMs, even as the Chinese have been expressing interest in such systems as TOW, HOT and Milan, they have been producing copies of the Sagger missile, the Soviet wire-guided ATM. While the TOW is far superior to the Sagger, it is also much more expensive and has roughly the same range (about 3 kms).

However, there have been reports of component sales to China --tank equipment, avionics packages, including heads-up-displays, fire control radars, and the like.[22] In any event, a two-tier system, consistent with the regime's economic reforms of decentralization, seems to have evolved--the more established ordnance and aviation ministries are handling negotiations that may lead to long-term technology transfer, while the newer corporations, like Polytechnic, are handling short-term, quick-fix purchases. But all of this would appear to conform to China's overall goal of "technological transformation." It is also in the tradition of incremental weapon systems improvement.

Such behavior suggests where the real, long-term interest lies. The army is not really in the market for hardware; rather, it wants the technology. A report in the September 23, 1984 issue of China Daily is quite candid on this score. Citing the views of a "high-ranking official" of the Commission of Defense Science, Technology and Industry, the paper reported: "China will continue to rely on its own efforts to develop its defense industry. However ... China is open to technological exchange (emphasis added) with the outside world to step up its defense modernization."[23]

Indeed, the Chinese perceive that they must master the technology problem in order to escape dependency on outside suppliers. Furthermore, Chinese officials are rather ambivalent about exactly what they can get from the West. In words startlingly reminiscent of the writings of the Chinese Self-Strengtheners one hundred years ago, Chinese Defense Minister Zhang Aiping warned in the March 1983 issue of Hong Qi:

> Our country is a big country and it is not realistic or possible for us to buy national defense modernization from abroad. We must soberly see that what can be bought is second grade. This cannot help us attain the goal of national defense modernization, nor will it help us shake off the passive state of being controlled by others. Depending or modeling one's weaponry on others is not a way of realizing national defense modernization either. At the onset it is necessary to obtain some technology that can be imported and model some weaponry on that of others. However, if we are content with copying, we will only be crawling behind others and still be unable to attain out anticipated goal. The fundamental way is to rely on ourselves. ... Only by developing--through self-reliance and in a realistic light--sophisticated military equipment that can be adapted to various conditions can we satisfy our Army's needs in its wars against aggression.[24]

But customer ambivalence and fears of receiving second-rate goods at the end of their product life cycle (not necessarily an unrealistic position) is not the only reason why the Chinese have been more active in the Western arms market. First, despite the policy decisions of high-level thinkers in Western capitals, there are substantial institutional barriers to weapons trade between China and the West. Any such deal would have to pass through domestic bureaucracies and COCOM--a process that, in the U.S. case at least, can take at least half a year just for civilian hi-tech products.

Furthermore, an arrangement between China and a Western arms supplier is, from the Western perspective at least, a business deal, and the Chinese simply drive very hard bargains. Profit margins are generally lower in business deals with China than they are when dealing with other countries; the Chinese usually demand a larger range of concessions than the firms are usually willing to grant; and despite the growing body of commerical law in China, including a patent law, the protection of technology and proprietary information remains a key concern of the Western business community.

Thus for all these reasons, it seems premature to declare China as a new market for Western military hardware or technology. Yet if China is to continue to modernize her forces, what obstacles and what policy implications does this drive have?

The Chinese answer, repeated <u>ad infinitum</u>, is "self-reliance." To be sure, this is a slippery term. But that it is the Chinese answer should recommend caution and modesty to China's would be suitors. "Self-reliance" also directs us to examine yet another aspect of the problem: how the Chinese see their own scientific and technological and weapon systems development process.

The Chinese Vision

Yang Shangkun, a Politburo member and Secretary General of the Central Military Commission, has published a number of authoritative commentaries on this subject. In connection with the 1984 Army Day, a <u>Hongqui</u> article under his by-line called for developing a "modern army with distinguishing Chinese characteristics." While China should learn from abroad, ("Anything useful for developing our troops should be taken over and utilized by us"), China should not blindly imitate ("We will always lag behind if we copy other people in modernizing our troops.").

Where does the army need to improve? By Yang's account, practically everywhere. He calls for rapidly developing "the most urgently-needed new types of weapons and equipment," new modes of organization, new doctrine ("we should carry on and develop Mao Zedong's military thought and develop new forms and combat methods of People's War under Modern Conditions"), and better troop training and indoctrination.

However, it is clear that all of this is subordinate to a political goal: "In order to deepen the reforms, our troops should thoroughly negate the 'Great Cultural Revolution', the influence of leftism and do away with the mentality of sticking to old ways and the desire to get things done once and for all." In other words, modernization is really a matter of reforming one's political outlook--everything else will follow from that.[25]

This political theme was reemphasized in a mid-September 1984 <u>People's Daily</u> article. Yang suggested that the army had gone through two phases of development and was now in its third--from being primarily an infantry force to an Army with air, naval, missile and engineering units and now to "a military force of combined talents." "The modernization of weaponry and equipment is an important ingredient of Army modernization," Yang continued. He not only listed the development of conventional and nuclear arms, but, in fact, stressed more recent developments in electronics, communications and missiles. "After the founding of the PRC, we experienced a process of first making replicas of weapons and then developing new weapons on our own. ... our Army can gradually and continuously renew and upgrade its weaponry and equipment."

But more important, it seems, "A new generation of military talent is growing up...The modern army is an area where new science and technology are highly intensive," Yang wrote. Thus, the Army needed a large number of talented military personnel who "have received a good education and have mastered scientific knowledge." He went on to laud the efforts of the many reestablished military academies, and claimed that since the Third Plenum of December 1978 which brought Deng back to power that "more than 1 million Army cadres" had been trained in them.

Education and political reform are closely linked, however. "It is still necessary to uphold the party's absolute leadership over the Army." Why? Yang was unusually frank: "As 'leftist' ideology is deeply rooted in the Army, the task of eliminating 'leftist' influence still cannot be neglected."

To be sure, Yang concluded, "Army building must be centered on modernization. ...If it is not modernized, it will find it difficult to fulfill the needs of modern wars. Its fighting strength will lack a material basis." But "the pernicious influence" of Lin Biao and the "Left" still "has not yet been thoroughly eliminated. ... Quite a few comrades are still fettered by 'leftist' influence." Yang concluded: "This situation must be changed as soon as possible."[26]

In other words, the regime puts military reform and modernization in the scope of the party and political reforms now sweeping the country. Political reform is a necessary precondition for further modernization of any kind, and Yang is serving notice that the PLA is not exempt. This has been echoed extensively elsewhere in the press. For instance, PLA Deputy Chief of Staff Zhang Zhen wrote on the eve of the 1984 Army Day: "It is not enough to have a scientific organizational system and to be armed with modern weapons and equipment. An even more important task is to train the kind of people who have lofty political consciousness and master advanced military thinking, modern scientific and technological knowledge, and modern weapons and equipment."[27]

Youth appears to be something of a factor here as well. An interview in the fall of 1984 with PLA political chief Yu Qiuli specifically linked new people with new ideas. Citing the youth and high educational standard of rising PLA officers, he said that "most" air force regimental commanders are "less than 30 years old" and "most of the officers at divisional and army levels are military academy graduates, while nearly all junior officers are college-educated." Yu concluded, "Talented, younger officers have helped advance the Army's modernization drive."[28] In other words, personnel policy is a major variable in defining what the Chinese mean by military modernization.

There are, to be sure, other issues in modernization. Military doctrine, treated elsewhere in this volume by Paul Godwin, is very important, for without a modern doctrine and a theory of application, weapons are mere hardware. "Warfare Under Modern Conditions" now means combined arms operations, a significant shift from the experience of senior PLA commanders.

Just where military modernization falls into the entire project of political and economic reforms launched by Deng is another major issue which we have only touched upon. One of the major themes here, dating, indeed, back to the founding of the People's Republic, has centered on relative development priorities. Essentially the question has been: Should military modernization take precedence over, occur simultaneously with, or follow, general economic development? The Deng regime has chosen the third option, and the relative polemical calm that has fallen over this issue suggests that, for the time being at least, Deng and his colleagues have carried the day.

Nonetheless, the regime has not ignored "the material basis" of military modernization. In preparation for the military review that took place on October 1, 1984, the article took some pride in detailing the "New Wings ... Added to A Fierce Tiger" as a late September 1984 People's Daily headline put it.[29] These include: creating an armored "ground shock force;" improved artillery, including advanced fire control and self-propulsion systems; nuclear submarines; a "new generation of high-speed fighters," and ICBM development.

In the same vein, China Daily cited a "high-ranking official" of the CDSTI as crediting the modernization of China's army to the application of high technology. This included a virtual laundry list of technologies, including "electronics, semi-conductors, infra-red and lasers in conjunction with optics, mechanics and electrical technology. Recent improvement in the precision of land forces ... is the result of research and application of automatic controls, laser and night vision technology and modern instrumentation."[30] Other articles on improved communications and fire control, with an emphasis on computers, are frequent. Be it rhetoric or not, there is a good deal of pride expressed in these commentaries.

Military Industries

Indeed, the regime takes considerable pride in the defense industry. There are many claims of new weapons development. One CDSTI official is cited: "China's defense industry, built nearly from scratch, has made remarkable progress in the past 35 years... the achievements are more obvious in the past five years after a series of reforms."[31] While there may be many questions, one cannot deny that China does produce a full range of military hardware, from pistols to ICBMs. In fact, Chinese political leaders have emphasized military technology as much as they have hardware. If we are to deal fully with the question of military modernization and weapon systems development we have to examine the industrial aspects of the question as well. While there is a lot of puffery about the military industries supplying "the Great Wall of Steel" as the PLA is sometimes tagged these days, there are other, more thoughtful pieces in the press as well.

One of the most interesting articles appeared in People's Daily just before the 1984 National Day military parade. The title of the piece evokes images of Socialist Realist art—"Battling on the Road to the Modernization of National Defense: On People Who Have Contributed to the Development of Our Army's Weapons and Equipment Over the Past 35 Years"—and its tone is relentlessly upbeat. But is it more than just a catalog of the progress and development of China's arms industry?

What distinguishes the piece is its historical perspective. It traces the development of China's arms industry back to the Self-Strengtheners of the mid-nineteenth century. While it is (of course) scornful of the failure of the arms industry to develop under the Qing and KMT periods and China's subsequent dependence on foreign arms, the article at least acknowledges that there are linkages with the past:

> In semifeudal and semicolonial Old China, due to corrupt governments and the backward economy and technology, it was impossible for the military industries to develop rapidly. From the establishment of the "imperial munitions factory" in Anging in 1861, the Qing Dynasty spent 16 years producing a simple and crude gun. Although the northern warlords and the KMT also set up some munitions factories, they could only manufacture backward firearms and ammunition, and they chiefly relied on "foreign firearms" to equip their soldiers.
> Following the birth of New China, our national defense scientists and technicians ... made overall plans for, rationally readjusted, and carried out the technological transformation of the munitions factories left over from the KMT and made them a starting point for further development. In a short time, they set up a number of large key enterprises, scientific research institutes, colleges and universities. They acquired knowledge while copying foreign products and then waged the battle of designing and developing their own new types of firearms.[32]

While no doubt the Soviets would not appreciate this condensed account of their 1950s aid to China, what we have here is an outline of what indeed seems to have been the developmental process of the Chinese arms industry. Perhaps more important, however, is the implicit example of this development through "technological transformation." This term is, in fact, one of the key slogans in the overall economic reform package of the regime. Upgrading established factories rather than creating new ones goes beyond domestic economics, however. It also appears to be an important strategy for funneling foreign investment. Thus once again this piece provides an example of the view that military modernization is part of the total Chinese modernization package. And it also suggests that should foreign suppliers become meaningfully involved with the Chinese defense market, they will probably be expected not only to transfer defense technology, but also to invest heavily in refurbishing existing plants.

Indeed, visitors to Chinese defense plants say there is a lot to be done. One engineer who visited several plants in 1984 told this writer that he was somewhat surprised at the high quality of the machine tools (all of the Chinese manufacture) and of the work being produced on them. At the same time, he said, he had a sense of being in a time warp, since all of the cutting tools were of designs modern three or four decades ago. He saw no numerically controlled tools, which are essential for producing modern weapons, or the most basic manufacturing environment controls. His observations coincide with those of other observers, who have termed Chinese high-tech production as being essentially at the level of "handicrafts."[33]

Linkage with domestic plans requires that we also look at the possibility of "tapping the potential" of the military industries for the civilian sector. This has been an important theme in industrial reform over the past several years. Essentially the argument has run that the military industries have excess capacity and relatively advanced equipment and technological knowhow. In the drive to increase civilian production, there has been a lot of press play on this topic. However, there are some indications that this trend may be winding down.

First, the exact contribution of the military industries to civilian production remains unclear. A CDSTI official has said that "civilian production made up twenty-two percent of the defense industry's total output,"[34] which is not insubstantial. However, we do not have statistics on the total output, both military and civilian, of the defense industries, nor do we know what percentage of total civilian production the defense contribution represents. In any event, the official noted, "priority lies in the research and production of new weapons."[35]

This last point is certainly similar to the emphasis given in an August 1984 article in Jingji Guanli (Economic Management) titled "The Strategic Question of the Arms Industry Developing the Production of Civilian Products." The strategy (since 1982) is to "give precedence to military goods" but also to "use the military to support the civilian." "The defense industries mainly serve the forces, but the amount of weaponry they require in peacetime is much different from that required in times of war."[36]

The intention, simply put, is to keep military production lines open in peacetime by manufacturing civilian products. Futhermore, there may be some technical spillover from the civilian sector to the military. But most important, particularly given the sweep of industrial reform in China today, is the potential for a "high standard of economic results"--that is, profits.

However, the article continues, there are problems. These are a litany of the kinds of industrial problems one can expect in bureaucratic state capitalism: a poor understanding of the market and hence wasteful use of resources; the inability to coordinate production; poor quality control; an unwillingness to play supplier to a final assembler; and an inability to stick to contracts and delivery schedules. Interestingly enough, one of the solutions proposed to solve these problems is that old standby, second-sourcing.[37] Indeed, the list is so complete that we can only conclude that the issues plague both defense production and the civilian-military output mix.

In fact, the regime appears to be addressing some of these larger issues, and despite the slogans, it knows where it stands. Zhang Aiping was very frank in a People's Daily interview that appeared just after the 1984 National Day celebrations. According to the reporters, Zhang "held that our national defense, though having made much progress in its modernization, was still lagging very far behind the national defenses of the developed countries and the countries that threaten our country's security." Although Zhang is unable to forego the almost universal political tendency to blame previous regimes for current problems (though he may be more justified than others), his solution to this lag is both inevitable and conventional: catch up through self-reliance and hard work.[38]

CONCLUSIONS

Our title posed a question, and we can only end with one. In this chapter, we have sketched some of the external and internal factors that have to be taken into account. What can we make of them?

First, it seems clear that the Chinese have clearly defined their threat environment. For the short term, they have deployed minimally adequate defensive forces. For the long term, military doctrine seems to be moving toward combined arms operations. Other necessary aspects of reform essential for continued modernization, particularly with respect to personnel, apparently are being implemented. In this connection, we should add that a very important Military Service Law which underlies much of this personnel reform effort is in accord with attempts in other sectors of Chinese society to regularlize and, indeed, institutionalize, programs and procedures. Overall the goal is the development of a military worthy of a great nation.

But big pictures examined up close have a tendency to dissolve into dots, and certainly this is so with respect to our topic. It is clear that it has developed a weapon system production base, and that the PLA is able to shift resources within that base to meet changing priorities--the Chinese nuclear and missile programs are examples. Yet given the paucity of resources, particularly of experienced engineers, shifts from one program to another can cause difficulties. For example, the big push to develop missiles apparently hurt the fighter program, and is thought to have significantly affected the J-7/MiG-21 project. Because of the Soviet legacy in inventory, design, and industrial organization, there are significant barriers to innovation and technology transfer. The "not invented here" syndrome, operative in all bureaucratic cultures, can only be reenforced by those factors.

Last, we have to take into account the Chinese cultural factor, because the system we have been examining here is more than just the sum of its history. The Chinese know where they are, and they know they have to "catch up." Whether a catch-up mentality condemns China to perpetual technological backwardness is an issue beyond the scope of this chapter. The real issue is whether the system now in place is adequate to China's needs.

Of course, only Chinese decisionmakers can determine how much is enough. While Chinese leaders seem to be aware of the problems confronting them, they also appear to be comfortable with their current defense efforts. One reason may be that there is more to the military environment than we have sketched.

One reading of Chinese history suggests a theme in Chinese political culture that tends simultaneously to downplay foreign threats and emphasize internal challenges. The Qing, though humiliated by foreign gun boats, saw in the Taiping and Nien rebellions the greater threat; Chiang Kaishek focused more on the tattered CCP than the Japanese invaders, and Mao, in the face of the United States in Vietnam and a Soviet build up, turned on his own party in the Cultural Revolution. The Chinese focus on internal order and the tradition of civil war was, interestingly enough, reemphasized in a Beijing Review article marking the 1984 Army Day celebration. Noting that the PLA "has become a regular, revolutionary army equipped with modern weaponry," the article noted its tasks: "Defending the people's political power, taking part in and safeguarding the socialist revolution, realizing the unification of the motherland, and protecting China from imperialist and hegemonist aggression."[39]

It is significant that only one of these four missions is externally directed; furthermore, that task is the last of the four. One would not want to put too much weight on this particular statement, but it does highlight the important, and perhaps peculiar, role the PLA has in domestic politics, and the domestic predilection among Chinese policymakers.

These factors combine with other issues examined above to explain why we do not see dramatic expressions of short-term urgency about the foreign threat facing China. These, plus the Chinese redefinition of the world order in the late 1970s and early 1980s (which suggested refocused and increased Soviet pressure on Europe)--itself a requirement of Chinese domestic politics so that the internal reforms could be implemented--begin to explain why China has been able to pursue a multivalent development strategy.

We still do not have, of course, a flow chart of the Chinese weapons decision process. But all of the factors we have examined suggest that despite the special characteristics of the PLA and the weapon system process, much of what we know about China in other areas can help explain what we see in the military sphere. The reverse of this also holds: military modernization fits into the other long-term reforms of the Deng regime. The current powerholders look out to the year 2000. For the short-and medium-term, structural constraints of the Chinese defense system, combined with cultural and historical factors, suggest that the Chinese will stay on a proven path: the incremental development, with aid from the West, of basically Soviet designs. Accomplishment of the longer term, greater national goals of the People's Republic remains, of course, less sure. But if modernization of technology and personnel continues, China will emerge less beholden to the past, and paradoxically, because of increased involvement with the outside world, more self-sufficient in the business of weapons development.

POSTSCRIPT

CCP Secretary General Hu Yaobang's April 1984 announcement that PLA conventional forces would be reduced by one million men in 1985 and 1986 (UPI, Arizona Republic, 20 April 1985) should be seen in the light of the Deng regime's attempt to streamline government operations. Chinese manpower reductions are not unexpected, given the pressure on older cadres to step down in favor of younger persons and scattered reports of PLA retirements. Also, we should not overlook the political context of the announcement. It was made during a visit to New Zealand at a time when Wellington was most concerned about the reduction of tension in the Pacific--so concerned that, indeed, the Lange government was involved in a dispute over port visits by nuclear-armed ships which threatened the ANZUS Pact.

Hu did not indicate where the cuts would fall, but it seems reasonable to assume that they would come mostly in the less well armed regional ground forces. Sizeable reductions in main force army units or in the more technically-oriented navy and air force, service arms which have increased responsibilities in combined arms operations and extended coastal (and off-shore oil) defense, seem unlikely.

We can get a better, if admittedly approximate, idea of how the cuts might be made if we look at how PLA manpower is allocated. According to IISS, of China's 4.2 million troops, about 80% are in the ground forces, 8% are in the navy, and 12% are in the air force. Taking the IISS Military Balance (1984-85) and the DIA Handbook (1984) numbers for the major (but not all) ground force units, we obtain:

Unit	Number	No. Troops	Manpower	% Manpower
Main Force Division	118	13,300	1,534,000	48.7
Armored Division (MF)	13	9,900	128,700	4.1
Artillery Division (MF)	33	5,800	191,400	6.1
Regional Force Division	73	7,500	547,500	17.4
Regional Force Regiment	140	2,200	308,000	9.8

Adding in a miscellany of railway, engineering, signal, chemical, adminstration and other units brings the total to about 3,150,000 for the ground forces.

While the precision of the numbers may be open to question, it is the relative distribution that is important. In this respect, the reduction could be made without compromising the main force units by cutting the regional forces. Indeed, some of the reduction may already be underway--IISS counted ninety-seven local force divisions in 1982. Also, some of the cuts may be obtained simply by reassignment--the transfer of local force units to the People's Armed Police would retain the unit while reducing the manpower account on the PLA's books.

NOTES

1. The author would like to thank Paul Godwin and M. C. Li for their perceptive and helpful comments on earlier drafts of this paper. See Richard Latham, "People's Republic of China: The Restructuring of Defense Industrial Policies," in J. E. Katz, ed., Arms Production in Developing Countries (Lexington, MA: Lexington Books, 1984), p. 109.

2. Foreign Broadcast Information Service, China Daily Report (hereafter referred to as FBIS), 1 October 1984, pp. K-1 - K-2.

3. See A. Preston, "The Changing Balance in the Pacific," Jane's Defence Weekly, 29 September 1984, pp. 547-551.

4. See the discussion in S. E. Johnson, The Military Equation in Northeast Asia (Washington, DC: The Brookings Institution, 1979).

5. See IISS, Military Balance 1984-85 (London: The International Institute of Strategic Studies, 1984), pp. 90-93.

6. See TO&E data in the Defense Intelligence Agency's Handbook for the Chinese Armed Forces (Washington, DC: Defense Intelligence Agency, 1976), pp. A2-A8, and Handbook of the Chinese People's Liberation Army (Washington, DC: Defense Intelligence Agency, 1984), pp. A1-A7.

7. S. B. Griffith, The Chinese People's Liberation Army (New York: McGraw-Hill, 1976), p. 178.

8. For additional information on the scientific and technical and defense industrial bureaucracy, see Latham, p. 109; Denis Fred Simon, "Rethinking R&D," China Business Review (July-August 1983): 25-31, and W. A. Fischer, "Scientific & Technical Planning in the People's Republic of China," Technological Forecasting & Social Changes (25): 189-207.

9. For attacks on the Fuzhou military industries, see FBIS, 5 February 1985, p. 01; for an example of what the Chinese mean by "unhealthy tendencies" see FBIS, 20 February 1985, p. K-8. For a

vivid account of the bureaucracy in action, see M. Oksenbert, "Economic Policy Making in China," China Quarterly 90 (June 1982).

10. A. J. Alexander, Soviet Science & Weapons Acquisition (Arlington, VA: The Rand Corporation (R-2942-NAS), 1982), pp. vi, 11.

11. See the discussion in Hans Heymann, China's Approach to Technology Acquisition: Part I--The Aircraft Industry (Arlington, VA: Rand Corporation (R-1573-ARPA), 1975), pp. 22-24.

12. See Fischer; and W. A. Fischer, "The Chief Engineer," China Business Review (November-December 1983).

13. FBIS, 18 September 1984, p. K-10.

14. Simon, p. 26.

15. See CONMILIT (Xiandai Junshi, Hong Kong), July 1984; and Jane's Defence Weekly, 23 June 1984, p. 1004. The London Sunday Times reported on 14 October 1985 that the 105mm gun is the English L7, but was provided to the Chinese by Israel. (FBIS, 16 October 1985, Annex 2.)

16. Jane's Armour and Artillery, 1982-83 (London: Jane's Publishing Co., 1982), pp. 135-136.

17. Private conversation with the author.

18. See for instance, C. A. Robinson, "Iraq, Iran Acquiring Chinese-Built Fighters," Aviation Week & Space Technology, 11 April 1983, and a similar story frontpaged in the Washington Post, 3 April 1984. Also see the report that 100 F-7s and 400-500 tanks were delivered by the PRC to Iraq in 1984, in Jane's Defence Weekly, 6 April 1985, p. 579.

19. Heymann, p. 19.

20. Private conversation with the author. The best technical article about this aircraft this writer has seen is in CONMILIT (November 1984): 10-11. According to an article in Interavia, China hopes to acquire navigation, radar, and missile systems for the aircraft. See "Aviation Expo/China '84," Interavia (1/1985): 159-161.

21. See, for instance, W. T. Tow, "Arms Sales to China," in G. Segal & W. T. Tow, Chinese Defense Policy (Urbana: University of Illinois Press, 1984). See also the reported British supply of laser and infra-red gear for the T-59 in Jane's Armour & Artillery, 1982-83, p. 2. See also footnote 16 above on Israeli military assistance to the PRC.

22. See D. F. Simon, "China's Capacity to Assimilate Foreign Technology: An Assessment," in *China Under the Four Modernizations* (Washington: DC: Joint Economic Committee, U.S. Congress, 1982), p. 535. For a discussion of similar patterns in a different service arm, see G. Jacobs, "China's Submarine Fleet," *Jane's Defence Weekly*, 9 February 1985.

23. *China Daily*, 23 September 1984.

24. FBIS, 17 March 1983, p. K-3.

25. FBIS, 1 August 1984, pp. K-3 - K-5.

26. FBIS, 18 September 1984, pp. K-2 - K-8.

27. FBIS, 21 August 1984, pp. K-18 - K-20.

28. FBIS, 14 September 1984, p. K-3.

29. FBIS, 24 September 1984, pp. K-5 - K-6.

30. FBIS, 24 September 1984, p. K-7.

31. Ibid.

32. FBIS, 5 October 1984, p. K-7.

33. Private conversations with the author in Beijing, 1984.

34. FBIS, 24 September 1984, p. K-7.

35. Ibid.

36. FBIS, 25 September 1984, pp. K-11 - K-18.

37. Ibid.

38. FBIS, 4 October 1984, p. K-2.

39. *Beijing Review*, 30 July 1984, p. 20.

6

The Reform of Military Education in China: An Overview*

William R. Heaton
Charles D. Lovejoy, Jr.

Since 1979, remarkable changes have been introduced in China's armed forces. The goal of the reformers headed by Deng Xiaoping is to build "a modernized and regularized Army with special Chinese characteristics."[1] Some of the reforms include the substantial reorganization of the command and control system of the People's Liberation Army (PLA); the retirement of senior leaders and officers, giving way to new leadership; and the reduction in the size of the armed forces. Last, but not least, a new spirit of professionalism has come to dominate the Chinese approach to military issues.

All of these things have been controversial and have encountered substantial opposition. Nevertheless, it is fair to say that the reform agenda has made substantial gains over the past seven years in coming to terms with the problem of how to balance the political indoctrination required to support the sacrifices of People's War with the technical training required to operate new weapons and command and control systems. As long as China's military development is technically and economically constrained, the PLA must rely on People's War, and this fact presents China's military leadership with continuing dilemmas over the relationship between military doctrine and political power and the problem of troop morale and motivation. So long as Deng Xiaoping and his supporters maintain the upper hand, progress in military reform will continue, although not uniformly or smoothly.

---

*Both authors have made extensive visits to Chinese Military Schools. Dr. Heaton visited the PLA Military Academy first in 1979 with a delegation from the National Defense University, the first U.S. military group to visit China. He visited again in the 1983 and 1984. Lieutenant Colonel Lovejoy, U.S. Army, was a member of the U.S. Military Education Delegation that visited China in May 1981.

A key component of the military reform agenda is to change and reform its educational system. China's military leaders believe that it will be difficult to make changes in weaponry, strategy, and organization unless the officer corps becomes better educated and more professional. As was stated by Xiao Ke, Deputy Minister of Defense and Commandant of the PLA Military Academy, "To run the Army well, it is first necessary to run the military colleges well."[2] This chapter is written to discuss how the reform agenda has affected military education in China.[3]

REFORMING THE SYSTEM

One of the principal reforms undertaken was to increase both the number of military academies and the number of personnel they could train. At the end of the Cultural Revolution, the military educational system was virtually in a shambles.

Chinese accounts now indicate that the decisions adopted at the 3rd plenum of the 11th Central Committee in December 1978, and more especially, since Deng became Chief of Staff of the PLA, started the process of rehabilitation. For example, the PLA Military Academy was reestablished in January 1978 after having been combined with the Political Academy from 1969. Other military academies also were being reestablished in 1978.

The movement for reform gained momentum in 1981 when Xiao Ke made two proposals to the Party Military Commission to restore rapidly the number of military academies and to improve greatly the educational level of the staff. In February 1983, the Military Commission convened a conference of high-ranking leaders from all the military academies. The conference endorsed the reform agenda and specifically criticized "left ideology" which obstructed reform.

The efforts of the reforms seemingly have been successful since, according to an article in Liaowang, the number of military academies has been increased to over 100 and "a relatively complete academy and school system has been formed to undertake the tasks of training, selecting and promoting, and recommending cadres for the Armed Forces."[4] The article further states that the number of military commanders and political commissars trained at academies and schools was gradually increasing. The official Chinese news agency Xinhua reported in July 1984 that the military academies had been organized into two categories: specialized technical schools and command schools. The specialized technical schools have intermediate and advanced levels. The intermediate level offers two-year courses on specialized technical and medical subjects, and the advanced schools offer three-year, and four- to six-year courses on various specialized subjects. The command schools have three levels: junior, intermediate, and senior. The junior schools train platoon commanders of various branches; the intermediate level schools train battalion level, deputy regimental level, and a small number of outstanding company level officers; and the senior schools enroll division level and a small number of outstanding regimental level officers.[5]

Recent figures reveal that more than a million officers have been trained at the academies since 1979. A report in May 1983 stated that the army would enroll 12,800 "outstanding fighters" in thirty military schools to train them as officers.[6] Beyond this, there has been a drive to recruit middle school and college graduates directly for training as officers. A report in July 1984 indicates that 1,600 college graduates had been appointed junior officers in the PLA after spending a year after graduation studying in military academies.[7] Prior to the military service law of 1984, officers had to come through the ranks. In 1982, the Military Commission decided that by 1985 over seventy percent of officers at the platoon level and above throughout the army should have undergone training in military schools and colleges. All naval ship commanders and air force pilots also must complete the requirement.[8] Two years later Han Huaizhi, assistant to the PLA Chief of Staff, reported that 96.5 percent of corps-level officers, eighty-seven percent of division level "leading" officers, and seventy-one percent of regimental "leading" officers had received training in military academies and schools.[9] This new requirement that officers have military academy training has greatly expanded the need for military academies.

Some of the physical facilities of the PLA Military Academy have been improved over the past five years. The academy has added new buildings and new equipment, including video training aids for classroom use. The naval academy also has acquired video equipment for classroom purposes. Physical improvements probably have been made at other academies. The Advanced Infantry School at Shijiazhuang, for instance, was newly built in May 1981 when visited by the U.S. Military Education Delegation.

Nevertheless, many of the facilities have yet to be significantly upgraded. The library at the PLA Military Academy, for example, does not appear to have changed significantly in the past five years. At the PLA Naval Academy, the students were using the red book--<u>Mao Zedong's Military Writings</u>--dated 1977 (a full year prior to the third plenum) as a basic text. It was interesting that they were reading Mao, then using that background to discuss the British campaign in the Falklands. When asked if some pictures, which obviously had been removed from the front of the text were pictures of Hua Guofeng (former Party Chairman and Premier), a student replied that he thought they were pictures of Lin Biao. When the date of the text was pointed out to him, he changed his mind and agreed they were probably Hua Guofeng! In any event, most of the material was similar to that commonly studied during the Cultural Revolution period, suggesting that many texts probably have not been updated.

REFORM OF THE CURRICULUM

As suggested by the above illustration, there have been some difficulties in updating the curriculum. The Chinese assure visitors that courses and research are constantly being improved to take into account the most recent developments on the battlefield. This assurance presumes access to information which, in fact, may be somewhat lacking.

Nevertheless, the spirit of curricular reform has been laid out in some of Deng's military writings and were canonized with the issuance of his Selected Works in 1983. In one such writing, "Streamline the Army to Raise its Combat Effectiveness," developed from a speech in March 1980, Deng states that all officers should attend military academies, that they should study modern warfare including strategy, and promotions should be related to their mastery of the material.[10] He also wrote that officers should study the works of Marx, Lenin, and Mao, as well as history, science, geography, foreign languages, mathematics, physics, chemistry, industry, agriculture, and other subjects. Deng further stressed that military education should not only prepare officers for more effective service in modern combat situations but also prepare them for civilian jobs when they retire.

Reform of the curriculum was a central theme of the conference on military academies held during February 1982. During the conference Xiao Ke identified four key problems among officers. Among these, the low level of scientific and general knowledge was listed as the highest problem. With proper education, Xiao asserted that the other three problems could be solved. Young officers would be able to succeed older officers; officers could be transferred to civilian work in the localities and officers could be exchanged and transferred among various services, arms, organizations, units, and schools.[11]

The major theme of curriculum reform has been to improve training in science and technology, strategy, and tactics in modern warfare. Generally speaking, the amount of time spent in political education and indoctrination has been cut back, with the possible exception of the political academies where ideology is a specialization. Citing Military Commission Vice Chairman Yang Shangkun, the Director of the General Political Department, Yu Qiuli, emphasized the importance of scientific and general knowledge in stating that, "the key to army modernization lies in skilled personnel. Without training a large number of modern military personnel, the modernization of the army is out of the question."[12] Yu further stated that those who wished to apply to military academies would be required to have a better knowledge of science.

A Beijing Radio broadcast in October 1984, which hailed the Military Academy as a "bastion of iron," observed that students must familiarize themselves "with this era of jet-propelled and nuclear weaponry." On no account should they "confine their thinking to the idea of millet plus rifles." It further observed that the academy tried its best to introduce the world's "modern scientific and cultural achievements and the fresh experiences gained from modern military campaigns."[13]

One of the principal internal obstacles to achieving these objectives is the lack of integration between the field and the classroom; another is the faculty. The Training Department of the PLA General Staff is responsible for the policy, direction, planning, and programing for training for all three services. The system is very centralized and there is little latitude for modification by subordinate elements down to and including the division level at various schools. The navy and air force seem to be much freer than the army about making proposals from below through higher headquarters to the Training Department. It is clear, however, that this centralized system needs revamping if it is to be a dynamic element in the development of new training programs and methods throughout the PLA.

While the General Staff places formal requirements on the schools, there appears to be little coordination between formal direction and school implementation. The result is a weak relationship between the operating force and military schools. Demands on the officer education system appear to be generated from within the schools. Central direction is reflected in school descriptions and determination of curriculum. There also is expected uniformity in the statements of political and professional objectives of each school. Service schools do provide input to combat units on various training plans or proposals but the connection is not an active one, certainly in comparison with that found in the U.S. training system. Because of this centralized system, the various schools do not feel they have an obligation for developing training materials for field units and the absence of a close association between the schools and the operating forces tends to sustain military education in a vacuum. Nor is there evidence of standardizing of training throughout the various service units. This appears especially true for the army, given its size, regional orientation, and the number of combat units involved. In addition, training in the PLA is very compartmentalized; regular force units, local force units, and the militia all have different programs.

The Military Academy, however, does play an indirect role in the development of PLA doctrine. While strategy is developed by the Military Commission of the Chinese Communist Party and doctrine is written by the Military Science Academy, actual writing of textbooks is done at the PLA Military Academy. The faculty has admitted that their study is complicated by the need for different strategies and tactics for contingencies against both the Soviet Union and Vietnam.

In the political academies the emphasis has been on the various ideological campaigns that have been conducted over the past few years. For example, the campaign in vogue at this writing is the one to "negate the Great Cultural Revolution." The political academies are presumably concentrating on how the themes of this campaign will be mastered by their students, and then transmitted throughout the armed forces.[14]

ISSUES

In 1983, Xiao Ke elaborated on three problems of professional military education which were posed by "the bondages of leftist erroneous thought." The first problem was the idea that previous military leaders had not had training in military colleges but had won victory anyway; some people argued that this fact made professional military education unnecessary. Xiao stated that this view was a wrong notion based on a misunderstanding of different historical environments and conditions.

The second problem was the common belief that officers who had formerly been students were not really capable of leading. To this, Xiao responded that many Chinese strategists, including Mao, had previously been students and cited Lenin to the effect that both modern warfare and technology required talent of high calibre.

The third problem was the argument that "Soldiers in our army come from the countryside, which has a low cultural level. Hence, the demand of the cultural level of cadres and staff members in the army cannot be too exacting. Moreover, since at present the degree of modernization in our army is not high, there is little use of demanding that army cadres must have training in military colleges." Xiao dismissed this argument as being shortsighted.[15]

The concern here is not so much for the relative merits of the arguments, but the fact that they have been raised at all. Clearly, some officers believe that renewed emphasis on military professionalism and the requirement for improving professional military education are threats to their status. No doubt their fears were reinforced by Yu Qiuli's statements that promotions should no longer be based on seniority, but on merit, further implying that training at a military academy was evidence of merit. Yu further asserted that the PLA must eliminate the barriers separating the armed forces and the military academies. This could be accomplished by selecting young, experienced, educated, and capable faculty members for promotion to leading positions in the armed forces.[16]

As a further reflection of the Chinese tendency to insulate education and professional development, education through the battalion and regimental command levels is conducted at branch schools. For example, the Armor School, which branched off from the PLA Military Academy in 1958 when it was in Nanjing, reports directly to the PLA Staff proponent for armor matters. So also does the newly formed Infantry School for mid-level commanders and cadres at Shijiazhuang.

The provision of schools for commanders at almost all echelons of command is an important feature of professional development in the PLA officer corps. The emphasis on regimental commanders and above, however, can be questioned in view of the notion that most of these commanders will have acquired important professional knowledge by this time. A more pragmatic reason for the large number of senior officers attending school may well be that the PLA simply does not "select out," and consequently there is an overabundance of senior officers without valid positions. In contrast to Western armies, the Chinese emphasize the education of senior commanders over the training of a large segment of middle rank officers who will be future commanders. The PLA believes so strongly in the power of the commander that it might have trouble with the proposition that commanders at the upper echelons need less training than middle grade staff officers. But this seems to be a central problem--the PLA has not built for its own future with a staff college system for the brightest and best of the upcoming middle grade officers.

The faculty situation in Chinese military schools is a reflection of two common problems in Chinese society: The "iron rice bowl" syndrome and the traditionally sharp division between abstract and practical knowledge. All faculty members appear to hold some form of tenured position, have been with their school almost their entire career, and have had little direct contact with the field. Most were selected for their special academic or technical skills and retained by virtue of the fact that they have held the job for a given period of time. Most also are military, although faculty members at technical and medical schools are mainly civilian. The existence of the iron rice bowl tenure system, however, somewhat obscures the distinction between military and civilian faculty members, particularly in many of the senior level schools, or in academically oriented courses at military academies.

The Chinese tendency to insulate professional development by specialty also is reflected in the treatment of military education faculty. While there appears to be no formal specialty code for instructors, the fact that they are teachers sets them apart. It is almost inconceivable that instructors would spend significant time in the field away from their instructional specialty. This fact also limits career opportunities and few faculty members expect to be promoted beyond their present rank. One exception to this general rule is the Infantry Command School. The teaching faculty consists almost totally of officers with troop experience, to include regimental, division, and corps commanders. Since it is new, the school does not have the long-tenure faculty found at other schools and faculty selection seems to be a high priority item for the commandant and his deputy. They have the authority to keep up to five percent of any class for the faculty and tend to pick the best. High ranking members of a school or academy who would be considered general officer equivalents do not teach on a regular basis. They, and leading regional commanders and cadre leaders, however, do lecture occasionally on appropriate subjects to set the tone and direction for specific issues (in other words, to set the party line).

With regard to academic credentials and the question of faculty prestige, it appears that the military school faculty have good credentials and enjoy a sense of prestige relative to their operational counterparts in the PLA. In relation to their civilian academic counterparts, however, they are clearly second class citizens. This fact is simply a reflection of traditional Chinese attitudes toward education, an attitude which is beginning once again to dominate Chinese thinking in general and influence individual decisions with regard to military service and military education.

While there are a host of technical issues that are relevant, for purposes of this discussion, it is sufficient to consider briefly the essence of the issues posed by Xiao. The first is that professional education is really irrelevant to command, and the second is similar in that it suggests that experience is far better than a textbook education in inculcating leadership. The third is a reversal of Xiao's proposition (or in other words, why have a professional military officer corps if China does not have a modern army and is not likely to have one in the foreseeable future).

Though Xiao dismisses them as "leftism," these questions really do effectively strike at the reformist postulations. It can be argued that Chinese defense policy and the present military system have served China reasonably well over the past thirty-six years. Incremental increases in capability will not enable China to make substantial gains on Soviet, or perhaps even Vietnamese, military might. The restructuring of the traditional ideological basis for esprit de corps to one based on professionalism could fundamentally alter the PLA in an undesirable way. The "leftists" are not without plausible arguments, though it should also be noted that their principal motivation is self-interest, since they are the ones who will lose as the reformist professionalizers gain.

But the trend seems clearly to be in favor of the reformers. Whatever the arguments, Deng and his supporters are committed to a thorough revamping of the military educational system, and they have already made considerable strides in doing so. In the areas of both structure and curriculum, there have been notable changes. In the future, we can expect that promotions will be more closely tied with professional military education.

At the 35th National Day celebration, (1 October 1984) the huge military parade in Beijing was led by officers of China's military academies. Perhaps no better symbol could serve as a reminder of the importance of military education to the future of China's armed forces.

NOTES

1. Yang Shangkun, "Building Chinese-Style Modernized Armed Forces," Hongqi (Red Flag) (1 August 1984); and Foreign Broadcast Information Service, Daily Report (China), 21 August 1984, pp. K-8 - K-18. (The FBIS materials will hereafter be abbreviated as DR/China.) In the article, Yang, who serves as Secretary General of the Central Committee's Military Commission, further states that, "To train modern military forces, the most important approach is to make the ranks of cadres more revolutionary, younger in average age, better educated, and more professionally competent."

2. Liu Huinian and Zhang Chunting, "To Run the Army Well, It is First Necessary to Run the Military Colleges Well--Xiao Ke on Building of Military Colleges," Liaowang (20 July 1983): 12-13; Joint Publications Research Service #4005/1101, pp. 72-77.

3. For earlier assessments see William Heaton, "Professional Miltary Education in China: A Visit to the Military Academy of the People's Liberation Army," China Quarterly (March 1980): 122-128; and "Professional Military Education in the People's Republic of China," The Chinese Defense Establishment, Continuity and Change in the 1980s, edited by Paul H. B. Godwin, (Boulder, CO: Westview Press, 1983), pp. 121-138.

4. "Interview with PLA Deputy Chief of Staff Zhang Zhen," Liaowang, no. 31, as carried by Xinhua, 29 July 1984; DR/China, 30 July 1984, pp. K-5 - K-6. This number compares with about 160 military academies before the Cultural Revolution.

5. Xinhua, 24 July 1984; DR/China, 25 July 1984, p. K-3.

6. Beijing Radio, 22 May 1983; DR/China, 26 May 1983, p. K3. According to a subsequent report, in the past thirty-four years 29,000 officers have received training at the PLA Military Academy. Beijing Radio, 4 October, 1984; DR/China, 9 October 1984, pp. K-8 - K-9.

7. Xinhua, 20 July 1984; DR/China, 23 July 1984, p. K-7.

8. Liu and Zhang interview with Xiao Ke, p. 77.

9. Xinhua, 24 July 1984; DR/China, 25 July 1984, p. K-5.

10. Xinhua citing Jiefangjun Bao (Liberation Army Daily), 4 June 1983; DR/China, p. K-33.

11. Xinhua, 22 February 1983; DR/China, 23 February 1983, p. K-31.

12. Xinhua, 23 September 1984, DR/China, 27 September 1984, p. K-1.

13. Beijing Radio, 4 October 1984; DR/China, 9 October 1984, pp. K-8 - K-9.

14. Jiang Siyi (Deputy Commandant of the PLA Political Academy), "Education in Totally Negating the Great Cultural Revolution Must be Conducted in a Down-to-Earth Manner," Beijing Radio, 2 September 1984; DR/China, 11 September 1984, pp. K-3 - K-9.

15. Liu and Zhang interview with Xiao Ke, pp. 75-76.

16. Xinhua, 3 March 1983; DR/China, 4 March 1983, p. K-2 - K-3.

7

Developments in China's Nuclear Weapons and Attitudes Toward Arms Control

Robert G. Sutter

INTRODUCTION [1]

As a result of strenuous efforts over the past thirty years, China has managed to develop a modest nuclear force, consisting of over 100 medium and intermediate range nuclear missiles, a few intercontinental ballistic missiles, aging bombers, and a submarine-launched ballistic missile that has undergone successful testing. Aided initially by the Soviet Union, China has developed it nuclear forces largely on its own. Chinese leaders have given the nuclear weapons program a consistently high priority and have generally managed to insulate it from the negative effects of the tumultuous political changes in China.

China's arsenal of between 225 and 300 nuclear weapons represents only a small fraction of the strategic nuclear forces of the United States and the Soviet Union, but it has given China some ability to deter Soviet aggression, to retaliate against a possible Soviet nuclear or conventional attack, and to enhance China's political influence in both Asian and world affairs. China's initial nuclear weapons development in the 1960s had a notably unsettling effect on the Asian balance of power. Despite the subsequent twists and turns in Chinese policy, however, Beijing has not engaged in "nuclear blackmail"--using nuclear weapons to threaten and intimidate non-nuclear neighbors--and Asian states have reacted calmly to recent Chinese weapons developments.

The implications of Chinese nuclear forces for American interests are mixed. On the one hand, a continuation of Beijing's gradual development of nuclear arms helps U.S. interests in maintaining a stable balance of forces along the Sino-Soviet frontier and helps check the perceived expansion of Soviet power and influence. But China's nuclear weapons also pose possible risks for U.S. interests. Thus, since a few Chinese missiles are now capable of hitting the continental United States with thermonuclear warheads, China might use its enhanced power to coerce its neighbors (for example, Taiwan and Korea) to follow policies favorable to Beijing. Additionally, China's possession of nuclear weapons has been a factor in prompting India to develop a nuclear weapons capability and Beijing reportedly has supplied nuclear weapons technology to Pakistan and certain nuclear materials to states engaged in furtive nuclear activities--charges which it denies.

CHINESE NUCLEAR FORCES

Chinese strategic nuclear weapons development dates back at least to the mid 1950s.[2] With extensive Soviet aid until 1959, as well as support from indigenous talent including repatriated Chinese scientists trained earlier in the United States, China was able to establish a sound base for future nuclear weapons development.

The withdrawal of all Soviet technical assistance in 1960 was a serious blow. Nevertheless, in the early 1960s, the Lanzhou gaseous diffusion separation plant began operation, assuring China a uranium enrichment capacity. Shortly thereafter, completion of two plutonium production reactors near Baotou, Inner Mongolia, allowed for weapons grade production. It is also noteworthy that China had adequate uranium supplies for this production of nuclear weapons materials.

With these assets and continued financial and policy support from the central government, Beijing's nuclear weapons program continued to progress steadily. In 1964, China detonated its first nuclear fission device, and in 1967, it successfully tested a fusion (thermonuclear/hydrogen) bomb. In 1966, China announced that it had fired its first nuclear-capable ballistic missile. Since the mid-1960s, nuclear weapons and delivery systems testing and development have continued apace. There has been an average of one or two major tests per year, although no nuclear testing has occurred since 1980. It is also significant that more than half of all Chinese military research and development funds between 1965 and 1979 were allotted to the nuclear weapons program.[3]

Thus, progress came despite shifts in Chinese policy and political instability including: the breakdown of political order during the Red Guard movement in the 1960s; the leadership purges during the Red Guard movement following the fall of Defense Minister Lin Biao in 1971, and after the death of Mao Zedong in 1976; and the shift in Chinese foreign and defense policy from emphasizing the U.S. threat to viewing the United States as a potentially useful counterweight to the Soviet threat to China.

Current Force Levels

Estimates of the size and organization of Chinese nuclear forces vary, but the available data and interviews with U.S. specialists point to a Chinese arsenal of between 225 and 300 nuclear weapons, including atomic weapons ranging from twenty to forty kilotons in yield, and thermonuclear weapons ranging from one to five megatons in yield. Delivery vehicles include land-based missiles and conventional bombers. A submarine-based ballistic missile has been successfully tested and will likely soon be deployed on China's first nuclear-powered ballistic missile-equipped submarine. The Chinese are reported to be continuing to increase their already significant stockpile of nuclear weapons material.

Chinese aircraft and missiles are among the most important aspect of this threat.

Bombers

Some of China's ninety TU-16 medium-range bombers, and perhaps some of its tactical aircraft, could be used to deliver nuclear weapons. However, these obsolescent aircraft would have great difficulty in penetrating sophisticated air defenses, and some observers speculate that it is improbable that China's air force has a strategic nuclear delivery mission against either the Soviet Union or U.S. forces in Asia.[4]

Ballistic Missiles

The Chinese have focused instead on developing and improving their missile delivery systems. This effort has resulted in several distinct land-based surface-to-surface systems, and the start of a sea-based system.

Medium Range Ballistic Missiles (MRBMs). China's MRBM forces consist of a small number (perhaps about fifty) liquid-fueled, single-staged, road-transportable missiles which are similar to earlier Soviet rockets. A 600-mile range missile, which has been operational since 1966, is believed to carry a nuclear warhead with a yield of twenty kilotons and is capable of striking some key military and industrial targets in the Soviet Far East as well as targets in Korea and Taiwan.

Intermediate Range Ballistic Missiles (IRBMs). China's IRBMs, operational since 1972, are also few in number (estimates range from fifty to eighty). These are powered by a Chinese-designed single-stage, liquid system, have a range of 1,500 miles, and carry a thermonuclear warhead having a yield estimated from one to three million tons by the International Institute for Strategic Studies. Deployment of this system provides China with a capacity to hit relatively large population and industrial centers in the central and eastern Soviet Union, as well as targets in East and South Asia.

Intercontinental Ballistic Missiles (ICBMs). In the early 1970s, China began testing a limited range intercontinental ballistic missile with a range of 5,000-7,000 kilometers (3,000-4,300 miles), and few of these have been reported deployed. Employing a multistage, liquid-fueled rocket, each missile carries a warhead estimated to have a three megaton yield, and can threaten targets in European Russia and all of Asia.

China's largest multistage ICBM was tested, with a substantial amount of publicity, with two firings in May 1980 from central China to the vicinity of the Fiji Islands, about 12,000 kilometers (7,450 miles) away. It is the only Chinese missile system capable of reaching targets throughout the United States and is thought to use liquid fuel and to carry a four to five megaton warhead. The London-based Institute for International Strategic Studies says China now has four of these missiles.[5]

Chinese land-based ballistic missile forces are thought to be targeted almost exclusively on Soviet territory and the available data indicates that at least the bulk of the Chinese missiles are deployed in northern and northwestern China and Tibet where they are in range of Soviet targets.[6]

Beginning in the late 1960s, Chinese missiles were deployed at a rate sufficiently slow that it did not alarm the Soviet Union, thereby provoking a Soviet "preventive strike."[7] The missiles were widely dispersed, often deployed in silos and man-made caves in mountainous terrain, and were so carefully camouflaged that satellite reconnaissance reportedly failed to disclose their presence until several years after they were initially deployed.

Meanwhile, pictures and news stories released by Beijing in 1979 indicated that some Chinese missiles are mobile by road and rail. As a result, an adversary might not be certain that it could locate and preemptively destroy all Chinese nuclear weapons sites during a conflict. On the other hand, it is widely held that Chinese reaction times are likely to be slow and, because of the time involved in preparing these missiles for firing, Chinese forces today are seen as incapable of launching much of an immediate retaliatory attack upon receiving warning of a surprise attack. They could have difficulty in responding quickly even after Soviet missiles hit Chinese targets, although some missiles could survive and be fired. Optimal preparation and dispersal of Chinese missile forces would appear to require a period of at least several days warning, such as would occur in the event of a rise in acute tensions with the Soviet Union.

<u>Submarine-Launched Ballistic Missiles (SLBMs)</u>. China's successful launch of an SLBM in 1982 no doubt has further complicated the strategic plans of likely adversaries and enhanced Chinese nuclear deterrence. In 1964, China successfully assembled a single diesel-electric-powered <u>Golf</u>-class submarine from parts supplied earlier by the Soviet Union. It has three missile launching tubes, is believed to be a testing platform, and presumably was the submarine that fired China's first SLBM in October 1982.[8]

China has also deployed a nuclear-powered submarine with twelve ballistic missile tubes. Submarines of this class could serve as the sea-based leg of the Chinese nuclear force of the future.

It is estimated that China's SLBM uses a solid fueled rocket and has a range of over 650 miles. The technology used in this missile--especially the use of a solid fuel rocket--could be applied to land-based missiles which would likely improve the mobility and reaction times of China's land-based forces.[9]

<u>Atomic Demolition Munitions (ADMs)</u>. Some specialists assume that Chinese nuclear forces include an unspecified number of ADMs. These devices are thought to be ready for use in the northern regions of China where they would be used to destroy mountain passes, divert rivers, and otherwise impede the progress of advancing enemy forces.

Prospects

It is widely held that because of its limited financial and technical resources, China will probably continue with the painstaking, incremental approach that has characterized its strategic nuclear weapons program of the past three decades.[10] Thus, China will presumably seek to keep pace with Soviet advances to some degree by improving the quality of its land- and sea-based missile forces, but would be unlikely to expand greatly the number of missiles or bombers needed to deliver nuclear weapons. Chinese leaders are expected to replace gradually some of the older liquid-fueled rockets with more mobile, accurate, and easily handled solid fuel weapons. China continues to devote a large portion of its scarce highly trained manpower and its government funds to nuclear weapons development and production.

Beijing may also have an interest in developing multiple reentry vehicles (MRVs) for its larger missiles. In 1982, one Chinese missile successfully launched three separate space research satellites, thereby suggesting a Chinese MRV capability. China is also thought to be interested in modernizing other capabilities related to its nuclear forces such as early warning radar, intelligence and reconnaissance satellites, more secure command and control equipment, better computers, and other instrumentation useful in producing and operating nuclear weapons.

There is some tentative evidence that China may be interested in developing battlefield nuclear weapons. Most notably, Chinese forces reportedly simulated nuclear warfare in a battlefield situation during a large military exercise in Ningxia province in north central China in June 1982.[11] Experts disagree as to whether this exercise was designed to strengthen Chinese defenses against an enemy using tactical nuclear weapons, or to simulate Chinese use of nuclear weapons in a tactical way against an invading enemy, or whether the exercise had another purpose.

Some specialists see China as particularly vulnerable to a large-scale Soviet conventional attack backed by Soviet tactical nuclear weapons. They claim that, without tactical nuclear weapons of their own, the Chinese would have to limit their nuclear response to strikes against targets in the Soviet Union-- an action that could lead to a large-scale Soviet nuclear attack on China. Nevertheless, others doubt that this apparent weakness will prompt China to develop additional tactical nuclear weapons.

They stress the weakness of China's command and control apparatus and the problems associated with maintaining central control over battlefield use of such weapons as reasons which discourage Beijing from additional weapons development.

CHINA'S OBJECTIVES

Few analysts see any immediate or substantial change in the goals of Chinese nuclear forces. Briefly put, these objectives have been, and are likely to remain:

--<u>to help deter Soviet aggression and intimidation</u>. This objective has been partly achieved since the Chinese have deployed a number of nuclear missiles capable of hitting Soviet targets. Because of Chinese use of mobility, concealment, and camouflage, and with the new Chinese SLBM capability coming into play, the Soviets probably judge that they cannot destroy the entire Chinese missile force even with a surprise attack.

--<u>to secure a strategic retaliatory capability</u>. This objective--which supports the first--says that China seeks a reliable and serviceable strategic retaliatory capability that could strike Soviet targets, should deterrence fail. This goal appears to have been at least partly achieved. The effectiveness of China's strategic retaliation remains constrained by Beijing's limited force size, and by the fact that some Chinese missiles will be destroyed by a Soviet preemptive strike because of the slow Chinese reaction and because of China's limited resources for obtaining adequate information on a possible Soviet attack. However, some Chinese missiles could survive a Soviet attack and could be used to retaliate.

--<u>to demonstrate China's international importance</u>. China has also developed nuclear weapons in order to enhance its influence in international affairs. It went far toward demonstrating its global strategic importance in 1980 when it became the third nation to test a land-based intercontinental ballistic missile successfully.

CHINA AND NUCLEAR ARMS CONTROL

China's position on nuclear arms control is influenced primarily by Chinese military weakness. Beijing has refused to limit its own nuclear weapons development as long as the United States and Soviet Union enjoy overwhelming advantages. Nevertheless, China has recently sought to soften its stance as an opponent of international safeguards for civil nuclear power, and of U.S.-Soviet arms accords. The Chinese want to enhance their international respectability, smooth the way for the purchase of nuclear technology, and encourage limits on the U.S.-Soviet nuclear arms race that jeopardizes Chinese security. Thus, while China still opposes the non-proliferation treaty, Beijing has recently joined the International Atomic Energy Agency (IAEA), publicly disavowed nuclear proliferation, participated in international disarmanent forums, and counseled on U.S.-Soviet arms restraint.[12]

In general, Beijing's policy toward arms control is governed by several important Chinese objectives. First, China wants to maintain its freedom in developing its nuclear capabilities against likely adversaries. For over the past twenty years, Chinese leaders have given a high priority to Chinese nuclear weapons development in order to help deter outside aggression and intimidation, to secure a strategic retaliatory capability, and to demonstrate China's international importance. Since the early 1970s, China's deterence and strategic retaliation capabilities have focused on the Soviet threat. Beijing has deployed over 100 missiles capable of hitting Soviet targets with nuclear warheads and has been reasonably sure that the Soviet Union remains unable to neutralize this force with a first strike against China.

Additionally, China wants to exert influence on the U.S.-Soviet arms control negotiations. In the 1970s, Beijing encouraged Western resistance to Soviet detente in the SALT talks, partly to avoid a decline in U.S. military pressure on the Soviet Union that would allow Moscow greater freedom in dealing with the China problem. In the 1980s, as Beijing has become less concerned about possible U.S.-Soviet collaboration against China, it has adopted a different tact, attempting to endorse a more moderate stance that both enjoys wider international support and fits well with China's regional security interests. China also sees the disarmament and arms control forums as useful platforms for projecting its image as the only developing country which has nuclear weapons, thereby underlining its position as a Third World leader.

In the 1960s, Beijing began criticizing the arms control negotiations as designed to maintain the superpowers' nuclear arms "monopoly." In the 1970s, as China emerged from its isolation, it believed that it was confronted with a possible U.S.-Soviet detente which would perpetuate China's inferior position. Thus, China was sharply critical of the SALT negotiations and accused the United States of attempting to "appease" the Soviets in order to divert the Soviet threat toward China.

During the late 1970s, China became even more concerned about Moscow's "unbridled" arms buildup, especially in Asia, claiming it threatened world peace and presented China with the problem of dealing alone with the Soviet Union--which it believed constituted its major security threat. Beijing thus called for a global "united front" against the Soviet Union, and moved closer to the United States and the West.

China perceived that the United States had adopted a stronger military stance in the 1980s in order to check the Soviet expansion, and it became less concerned about a possible U.S.-Soviet rapprochement at Chinese expense. The only exception to this trend occurred in 1982-1983, when it appeared that the two superpowers might reach an agreement on intermediate force missiles that would have allowed Moscow to redeploy its SS-20 missiles from Europe to Asia. However, the Chinese were reportedly reassured of U.S. intentions, and, as the U.S.-Soviet talks broke down, China shifted its attention to the negative implications for China of the superpower arms race. Thus, by 1983, the Chinese media persistently highlighted the dangers of the U.S. and Soviet arms buildups, and retreated from its earlier criticism of the arms reduction talks.

In part, China's position was based on basic security concerns. The Chinese were preoccupied with what they increasingly perceived as an accelerating U.S.-Soviet arms race that had led to an increase in Soviet forces in East Asia and a widening in the gap between Soviet and Chinese military capabilities. China hoped to focus on economic modernization and to avoid the increased defense spending needed to keep pace with Soviet progress. In the interim, to avoid domination by Moscow, China was forced to compromise with and establish closer ties to the United States. Thus, the Chinese saw the arms race as entering a new stage that would leave China militarily further behind the United States and the Soviet Union. This threatened a greater bipolarity in world politics, making it more difficult for China to steer an "independent" foreign policy course.

At the same time, a moderate anti-superpower line has fit well with the contemporary Chinese image in the international arena. Thus, China's arms control proposals at the U.N. disarmament conference in 1982 and the U.N. General Assembly in 1983 focused on a position that called for the two superpowers to stop all testing and research of new nuclear weapons, and to agree to cut their stockpiles in half. If this pledge were made by Moscow and Washington, then Beijing would declare its willingness to attend a world disarmanent conference.

China obviously has little expectation that its proposal will win approval, but it serves to focus critical attention on the superpowers in a way that will please the broad ranks of the international peace movement. This line was also behind Premier Zhao Ziyang's support for the European peace movement during his trip to the continent in June 1984.

NOTES

1. This article is based on a review of available unclassified literature and other data, as well as a series of interviews and consultations conducted with fifteen U.S. Government and non-Government specialists knowledgeable about Chinese nuclear weapons and their significance for U.S. policy. The views expressed in this paper are those of the author and do not represent the views or positions of the Congressional Research Service.

2. For background on Chinese nuclear forces see The Military Balance, 1983-1984 (Washington, DC: Defense Intelligence Agency, Handbook on the Chinese Armed Forces); Harlan Jencks, From Muskets to Missiles (Boulder, CO: Westview Press, 1983); Ian Johnston,

Chinese Nuclear Force Modernization and Its Implications For Arms Control, unpublished manuscript, 1983; Garrett Banning and Bonnie Glaser, Soviet and Chinese Strategic Perceptions in Peacetime and Wartime, unpublished manuscript, 1982; and Garrett Banning and Bonnie Glaser, War and Peace: The Views From Moscow and Beijing (Berkeley: University of California Press, 1984).

3. See, Central Intelligence Agency, Chinese Defense Spending, 1965-79. See also, U.S. Congress, Joint Economic Committee, China and the Four Modernizations (Washington, DC: U.S. Government Printing Office, 1982), pp. 597-610.

4. See for example, Jencks, p. 158.

5. The Military Balance, 1983-1984, p. 84.

6. See Jencks for background on the deployment of Chinese missiles.

7. Ibid.

8. See David Muller, "China's SLBM in Perspective" in U.S. Naval Institute Proceedings 109 (March 1983): 125-7, for background on Chinese developments in this area.

9. The advent of an operational Chinese SLBM will increase the perceived danger that Chinese nuclear forces might somehow provide the catalyst for a U.S.-Soviet nuclear exchange. There is some doubt, for example, as to whether or not the Soviet Union could identify accurately an incoming Chinese missile, particularly an SLBM. If Moscow thought it were an American missile, it might retaliate, leading to U.S.-Soviet nuclear conflict.

10. For background, see U.S. Senate, Committee on Foreign Relations, The Implications of U.S.-China Military Cooperation (Washington, DC: U.S. Government Printing Office, 1982).

11. Cited in Johnston, p. 12.

12. For an extensive survey of issues related to China's new interests and participation in arms control issues, see David Salem, The People's Republic of China, International Law and Arms Control, occasional paper/Reprint Series in Contemporary Asian Studies, no. 6 (College Park, MD: School of Law, University of Maryland, 1983).

8

Summary: China's Military Modernization: A Systemic Analysis[1]

Robert E. Johnson, Jr.

INTRODUCTION

The Chinese leadership, under the guidance of Deng Xiaoping, has committed itself to a policy of reform, an action which, according to all reports, is aimed at producing profound change in the Chinese economic, political, and defense systems. As with almost all reform programs there are a number of outcomes and implications, some of which are intended, and some which are not. Sometimes unintended implications are foreseen and subsequently accomodated by containing their effect. More often, however, unintended outcomes are unforeseen and create conditions conducive to political instability. Such outcomes are the stuff of the development studies pursued by a number of political scientists. Sometimes outcomes and implications are not only unintended and unforeseen but also are not readily or easily identified.

The preceding chapters of this book have identified some of the implications of China's attempt to modernize its military establishment. To a large extent the authors have focused on the intended outcomes of Chinese policies and have offered their assessments of the relative ease or difficulty with which these policies are likely to achieve their objectives. However, for two reasons, the unintended implications largely have been left unexplored. First, it is often very difficult to determine the intended outcomes of specific Chinese policies. While information from official sources has proliferated in recent years, a great deal of secrecy still surrounds the Chinese military. Secondly, although the decision to reform and modernize the People's Liberation Army (PLA) was made in 1978, it has been only within the last two to four years that the outline of the basic policies has become apparent to Western analysts, and more time is needed to assess all the implications of these reforms.

The purpose of this chapter, therefore, is to synthesize the conclusions of the previous chapters and to identify the systemic implications of these conclusions. As Charles Lovejoy pointed out in the foreword, Chinese military modernization influences two different systems. First, there is the influence that modernization has upon the internal characteristics of China--that is, the political decisionmaking process and worldview of the Chinese elite. Second, there is the influence modernization has upon the role China will play in the world system. This theoretical divide is bridged by the fact that the Chinese elite's perceptions of their role in the international system will affect the role China does assume. Therefore, there is an implicit connection between the impact reform will have on the Chinese system and the effects the same reforms will have upon the international system.

However, before investigating these implications it is useful to review the background against which these reforms are being implemented. The most basic element of the Chinese defense reform program is the fact that military modernization is the last priority of the four modernizations. In real terms this means that the armed forces no longer can rely upon receiving the most qualified technical personnel or an inordinate share of the limited financial or material resources. Instead, the leadership has emphasized modernizing the civilian economic system with the implicit understanding that, as the industrial base modernizes, so will the defense establishment. Therefore, while the PLA can depend upon continued support for its operating and maintenance needs, the defense establishment can expect only limited support for its modernization programs. These priorities have led to the fundamental nature of current defense reform policies which are oriented toward changing the way armed forces' personnel think about and organize for the defense of China. In short, current defense reforms are aimed at modernizing the people in the armed forces rather than the equipment.

Of course, the foregoing somewhat simplifies reality--the military still retains a sizeable research and development establishment which seeks to provide modern equipment to the armed forces. However, the emphasis in the current military reform policy is to revamp the personnel, organizational, training, and educational policies of the past.

These reforms have not been implemented without debate. In fact, the most organized and entrenched opposition to Deng Xiaoping's policies has come from old conservative PLA leaders, who have fought to preserve their bureaucratic positions in the face of programs seemingly designed to retire them. However, as William Heaton observed, there are plausible conservative arguments as to why some of the reforms are either not needed or detrimental to the Chinese defense effort.

Therefore, it should be recognized that while the reformist policies appear to have been adopted by the Chinese leadership, there remains political and military opposition to these reforms. Furthermore, it is very difficult to gauge the depth of this opposition, thereby making it possible, even if unlikely, that future events might cause a reversal or modification of these policies.

INTERNATIONAL SYSTEMIC IMPLICATIONS

In recent years two paradigms have dominated the study of the international system: the balance of power and the interdepedence theories.[2] While each has provided insights into the understanding of how the world system functions, neither has proven to be totally comprehensive in explaining world events.

Power Politics Theory

The balance of power theory (or power politics) is based on the argument that, in an anarchical, hostile world in which conflict is the norm, states pursue power. Nations seek an equilibrium in the distribution of power among states that will result in a stable world system which thereby insures the security of member states. The international system is described in terms of the number of powerful states (or poles) that dominate the system. Hence, the terms bipolar, bipolycentic, tripolar, and multipolar are used to explain varying perceptions of the distribution of power. It should be noted that due to the relative nature and the intangible aspects of measuring power, there still remains substantial room for disagreement among power theorists on the nature and shifting of the balance of power.

The power politics approach when applied within the context of this book focuses on the impact PLA modernization will have upon China's relative power and, therefore, upon the regional and world power balance.

This approach in assessing Chinese military modernization is implicit in the fears of ASEAN leaders which William Tow describes as well as in the concerns that have been expressed by the Soviet Union, Taiwan, and conservative leaders in the United States. The basic concern focuses on the wisdom of encouraging Chinese military modernization. Of course, such concerns theoretically would be resolved if we felt assured that a more powerful China would be a friendly China. However, as William Tow indicated, Chinese self-interest has instilled a national dimension to Deng Xiaoping's objectives of PLA modernization; that is, the creation of a non-aligned, independent, and strong China. Given this Chinese orientation, adherents of the power politics approach feel justified in closely assessing the ramifications of assisting the Chinese in the PLA's improvement.

In the preceding chapters two observations suggest interesting balance of power implications. Robert Sutter has noted that the Chinese are increasingly willing to discuss arms control issues. The power politics approach would suggest that this indicates a Chinese perception that arms control can affect their relative power in the world system and, therefore, increased Chinese involvement in arms control organizations would be wise.

More specifically, political realists argue that diplomacy is one component or tool in the exercise of a state's power. Robert Sutter notes that China's diplomatic shift on disarmament enables the Beijing leadership to maintain freedom in developing its nuclear capabilities while exerting influence on the U.S.-Soviet arms control negotiations. In doing so, he implicitly accepts the notion that Chinese diplomacy is pursued to enhance relative Chinese power.

Richard Latham notes an increased Chinese willingness to compete in the growing commercialization of arms transfers, which has led to sales to Third World nations, most notably Iran and Iraq. While Chinese sales are at the "low-tech" range of the spectrum, they conceivably could affect regional power balances in sensitive areas of the world such as the Middle East. This is a significant international aspect of China's drive to modernize since these sales are attempts to raise foreign capital to assist in the modernization process. Xia Wenxiang's statement that all Chinese products are for sale with no strings attached indicates not only a willingness to sell arms, but also the possibility that current regional power balances could be challenged.

Interdependence Theory

The interdependence theory assumes that the superpowers are locked into a stable nuclear stalemate. This has resulted in the relative increased importance of "low political" issues such as economics and welfare, which have supplanted the formerly decisive "high political" issues of security. Advocates of the interdependence approach claim that under such circumstances states have found that in "low political" issues they have common interests. This leads to replacing conflict with cooperation as the dominant type of interaction among states in the world system.
When applied to China, this approach implicitly emphasizes the economic and cooperative aspects of providing military aid to the People's Republic of China. There are two lines of argument. First, as William Tow has pointed out, China has realized that the West is its only real source of modern weapons technology. The interest in the West's technology has resulted in increased contacts, agreements, and trade which promote shared interests and, therefore, greater cooperation between the West and China. Secondly, as the Chinese study Western concepts they inevitably are influenced by some Western attitudes which leads to a greater perception of shared interests and cooperation. Both of these points are implicit in noteworthy Japanese, Western European, and the American liberal views.
In the preceding chapters a number of noted developments suggest interpendence implications. Robert Sutter's observation of China's increased willingness to seriously discuss arms control could possibly be a result of recent Chinese scholarly studies of Western works on arms control.[3] These studies might have caused some Chinese leaders to realize the shared interests of arms control and therefore have led to a more cooperative attitude. Additionally, as Sutter points out, Chinese arms control proposals represent a moderate anti-superpower line that can be justified from the interdependence viewpoint of the international peace movement. Therefore, while Sutter's power politics-based analysis of the Chinese arms control policy is persuasive, an interdependence-based justification of the policy cannot be ignored.

Wendy Frieman and Richard Latham present notions which together may explain increased Chinese arms sales using the interdependence approach. These arms sales appear to have been pursued to secure foreign exchange which will enable China to increase purchases of Western technology. Such sales could lead to greater contact and cooperation with the West.

Paradoxically, this growth in interdependence could lessen the possibility that Chinese arms sales could upset regional power balances. Such a growth could occur through a greater Chinese awareness and commitment to the status quo that is engendered by its reliance upon a stable international system and market to support its modernization.

William Heaton and Paul Godwin infer that the PLA's close study of modern warfare has led it to examine Western military theory and organization. These studies have contributed in part to PLA personnel and educational reforms, as well as to changes in military doctrine. Such an influence, according to the interdependence theory, should lead to greater cooperation with the West.

William Tow posits the interdependence approach most clearly when he suggests the possibility that Western technology transfer to the Chinese could be a long-term instrument of persuasion, since it strengthens political relations and softens ideological schisims.

On the other hand, John Frankenstein identifies three barriers to Sino-Western interaction that could limit the applicability of the interdependence approach. First, the long lead times for COCOM approvals of Western high-tech sales to China hampers military trade. Second, Chinese organizations tend to drive excessively hard bargains with Western companies, causing many to avoid such trade. Lastly, many Western companies remain concerned over disseminating techniques or information to the Chinese.

While Beijing has tried to calm Western concerns about the release of information through promulgating new commercial laws, many Western companies remain leery of doing business with China. On the other hand, the first two barriers represent a "learning curve" which must be "ridden" before Sino-Western trade relations can fully develop, and the question remains as to how willing Chinese and Western leaders are to "ride the curve."

William Tow reminds us of the result of the Soviet attempt to control their technology transfer to the Chinese in the 1950s. While the obvious alternative is to not control, such a policy is not likely, because it would require Western leaders to completely reject the balance of power approach, and this would entail unacceptable international and domestic political risks.

Strengths and Weaknesses of the Two Approaches

As noted earlier, both paradigms have their strengths and limitations. Conventional wisdom holds that the balance of power theory is applicable to security issues while the interdependence theory best explains international economic and trade policy issues. However, this distinction is not clear cut. Competitive trade policies among nations can be explained, at least in part, as an attempt by states to gain economic power, which enhances their relative power. On the other hand, efforts at arms control indicate cooperative attempts at solving, or at least alleviating, the greatest security issue of our time. Therefore, not only do the two paradigms fail to comprehensively describe international systemic trends, but also they cannot be presented as comprehensive explanations of categories of issues of the world system.

What can be safely stated, though, is that the assumptions implicit in either theory will necessarily lead an advocate of one system to view the implications of Chinese military modernization quite differently from an advocate of the other. However, it appears that realizing the limitations of both theories must be kept in mind when applying either. Such a notion is inherent in William Tow's and John Frankenstein's discussions of COCOM. COCOM can perceive trade with China from a power politics or from an interdependence approach, or can shift between the two perspectives depending upon the circumstances. How COCOM handles the China trade policy issue will indicate its attitudes and therefore will have a marked impact upon Sino-Western relations.

Likewise, how the Chinese perceive the international system and what theories they use for making policy decisions will affect Sino-Western relations. Although Western power politics and interdependence theories fail to adequately describe Chinese analytical frameworks concerning the world system, elements of these two approaches historically have been present in Chinese foreign policy. Anyone who has read <u>The Romance of the Three Kingdoms</u>, studied the internecine political struggles within the Chinese Communist Party, or studied the Chinese rationale behind rapprochement with the United States in the 1970s has realized the prominent role power politics plays in the Chinese political system. Likewise, anyone who has followed Chinese foreign policy over the last three decades cannot help but realize the interdependence theme of Chinese policies such as "the five principles of peaceful coexistence."

In such a fluid international environment, the only definitve statement that can be offered is that there are international implications to Chinese military modernization. Robert Sutter and Richard Latham have noted two such implications. The explanations behind these implications are, on the one hand, the essence of analysis and, on the other hand, the subject of debate.

DOMESTIC SYSTEMIC IMPLICATIONS

Jonathan Pollack has noted that Chinese military studies' "most conspicuous inadequacy... (is) its almost total lack of analytical context."[4] While Harlan Jencks and Harvey Nelson have provided substantial contributions to understanding the PLA, their works have done more to expand what is known about the

Chinese military than to develop a comprehensive analytical framework for further study.[5] There are good, salient reasons for this lack of analytical context in Chinese military studies, not the least of which is the difficulty in retrieving and collating reliable information on which to base indepth analysis.

Given this situation, it is not surprising that there is no systemic model upon which to base an analysis of the domestic implications of Chinese military modernization. The task of performing such an analysis becomes more difficult when one considers the issue of how to define the boundaries of the Chinese domestic system and what components of that system should be included when considering the implications of PLA modernization. Therefore, it is with the awareness of the substantial limitations of this type of analysis that the following organizing themes are used to describe domestic systemic implications.

Change Within the PLA

Change within the PLA can best be described by focusing on the cleavages within the Chinese military that previously have been identified by Chinese scholars.[6] Such an analytical framework focuses on conflict within the PLA as the organizing theme for understanding implications of current policies.[7]

Maoism Versus Professionalism

As William Heaton notes, professionalism is now emphasized in the PLA. This is evident in military personnel recruitment and educational reforms and in the codification of the Military Service Law which regularized and institutionalized personnel reforms within the PLA. Additionally, as William Tow points out, while ideological ambiguity concerning the administrative power and upward mobility of technocrats vis-a-vis the political cadre remains, emphasis within the PLA (and in China as a whole) has been upon upgrading the status of technically proficient personnel. Finally, as Paul Godwin and William Heaton note, political education has been devoted almost exclusively to "negating the Great Proletarian Cultural Revolution" and combatting "leftism," both slogans for eradicating the more radical aspects of what Western analysts refer to as Maoism.

However, while professionalism is currently emphasized in the Chinese high command, there remains concerns and, in some cases, opposition to deemphasizing Maoist principles. These concerns have been articulated by the surviving marshals of the 1950s: Ye Jianying, Nie Rongzhen, and Xu Xiangqian, who have been active in insuring that Maoist principles continue to influence policy issues such as the restoration of ranks, the strategy of People's War, and the importance of the militia in the defense of China.[8]

These marshals have been described as advocates of military professionalism when compared to the policies of Maoist radicals such as the "gang of four;" but, when compared to the policies of the pragmatic Dengists, these older soldiers seem to become more Maoist in orientation. In both cases the older military leaders have acted as a brake against policies that sought to radically change the status quo within the PLA. Therefore, while the Maoist vs. professional cleavage does help to explain changes within the PLA, it does not account for all the changes occurring within the Chinese Army. In a sense, both the Dengists and Maoists can be described as radicals seeking to drastically change the status quo while the marshals represent that portion of the PLA which seeks a slow, evolutionary change.

Interpersonal Associations

While William Whitson's field army model of the PLA has been shown to be less than totally reliable, it does form the basis upon which to begin understanding the importance of personal relationships in the Chinese military.[9] For instance, the fact that Qin Jinwei (commander of the Beijing Military Region), Yang Dezhi (Director of the General Staff Department), and Liu Huaqing (commander of the PLA Navy) are all former members of Deng Xiaoping's 2d Field Army is not overlooked by most PLA analysts. Still, the argument that current PLA policies are shaped by alliance systems formed over thirty years ago is tenuous at best.

Perhaps a more significant distinction is Whitson's comments concerning the generations of PLA leaders. As pointed out in previous chapters, the "old guard" of the PLA has been slowly passing away over the last decade. Conversely, Harvey Nelsen has documented the frustration and resentment that the field grades and lower ranking generals have felt over their limited opportunities for advancement.[10] This cleavage among generations of PLA leaders has been addressed by Deng Xiaoping in those policies intended to induce or force the retirement of the older cadre. Resistance to these policies has been substantial and only within the last two years have significant numbers of retirements occurred at the division-level and above. Paul Godwin has already noted that this resistance has been based partly upon the older cadres' concerns over the pace of reforms and largely upon their fear of loss of status.

Despite the difficulty in inducing older PLA cadres to retire, the current policy is likely to succeed. Hence, generational conflict within the PLA is likely to become less of an issue in the future, assuming that the announced decision to implement standardized retirement ages and procedures is carried out.

No discussion concerning Chinese interpersonal associations would be complete without consideration of factional politics. The promotion system within the PLA has led to the difficult problem of "mountaintopism", which is the creation of vertical factions that compete for high-level positions.[11] While this phenomenon was the basis upon which the field army model was constructed, the limited tenability of Whitson's theory has not changed the fact that "mountaintopism" has remained a concern of the Chinese leadership.

The PLA promotion reform proposals have emphasized technical expertise as a key criterion in selecting officers for high level positions, failing to focus on those aspects of the promotion system that engender the formation of cliques. The reason for this lies in the stability, cumulative experience, and high espirit de corps that the current system provides.[12] Instead, the problem of PLA factionalism is handled through periodic transfers of top regional and district leaders and through sending future military leaders to centrally run military schools. While such actions clearly do not prevent the creation of PLA factions, they have been deemed an appropriate compromise between the advantages of the PLA promotion system and the factions it creates. Therefore, factional politics is likely to continue to contain some explantory power in understanding PLA personnel and policy changes.

Institutional Structure

Vertical cleavages exist between institutions of the PLA. These are largely a result of a profound lack of horizontal lines of communication that has resulted from the organizational structure of the military bureaucracy and from the role vertical cliques play in the PLA. Such isolation between groups of PLA institutions inevitably leads to duplication, inefficiencies, and a lack of standardization. Despite identification of this critical problem, there has been very little evidence of any attempt to alleviate it.

William Tow struck the heart of this problem when he questioned how spillover effects would occur between economic sectors without horizontal lines of communication. The significance of this dilemma increases when we consider that the PLA has been relegated to the last of the four modernizations.

In fairness it should be noted that Beijing has indicated its awareness of this problem. Therefore, reforms oriented toward increasing the ability and incentives of PLA managers and leaders to communicate between organizations are probably under development and testing. Research needs to be done in this area to identify and analyze these reforms.

A related, but somewhat contradictory, concern of the party leadership is the continued central control of the PLA. The historic fear of Chinese rulers has been the development of strong, semi-autonomous regional rivals. This fear has been addressed in the PLA organizational structure by reserving control over main force units to the central leadership. This compartmentalization of control between main force and regional units is especially important given the fact that military region commanders and political commissars often hold concurrent policy-making roles within the corresponding provincial or municipal party organizations.

Thus, there is a perceived need by the Chinese leadership to balance the requirement for enhanced horizontal communication with the imperative of reserving ultimate authority for the central rulers. The importance of achieving this balance cannot be overemphasized given the Chinese cultural propensity to recognize authority derived through personal associations and commitments over that derived from organizational role or structure.

Sectoral Differences

The study of intra-military behavior of developing states indicates that inter-service rivalries are good predictors of policy preferences and budgetary allocations. These rivalries can only be inferred in the Chinese case as direct evidence of such conflict is rarely available. Such rivalries are inferred from debates over alternative strategic posture and modernization programs and from available evidence on existing military capabilities. The "electronic vs. steel" debate of the early 1970's, the "People's War under Modern Conditions" debate of the late 1970's, and the growth of the Chinese nuclear arsenal are classic examples which indicate likely areas of rivalry between the PLA services. These theoretically should become more intense now that China has committed itself to modernization while relegating the military a low priority in resource allocation.

Another indicator of inter-service rivalries could well be the decisions the Chinese have made concerning purchases of foreign military hardware. Cancellation of the Luda-class destroyer refitting and the Chinese Air Force's difficulty in securing the high command's approval for British Harrier and French Mirage aircraft purchases indicate a reluctance to purchase high-cost items and competition for scarce foreign currency to fund such purchases.

Although the navy and the air force will continue to seek a strategic role for themselves, both services will likely remain adjuncts to the PLA ground forces. Given the projected slow pace of modernization, the debates among services will be subordinated to the more important decisions concerning resource allocation. Therefore, despite the theoretical likelihood of the rivalries increasing in the coming years, such conflicts are unlikely to provide an adequate analytical framework from which to understand changes within the PLA. Nevertheless, this aspect requires more development through additional research.

Systemic Change of the PLA's Role Within China

Two roles of the PLA are important in assessing the implications of Chinese military modernization: the PLA as a political actor and its role in Chinese society.

Political Actor

To explain that the low priority assigned to military

modernization is due to a loss of political clout is too simplistic. The Chinese military still commands a sizeable percentage of the state budget and continues to fund a large defense industry.[13] Additionally, a significant part of the Chinese Communist Party Central Committee is made up of PLA officers.[14] A more likely explanation is that the PLA has accepted the lower priority in exchange for other concessions.[15] These are likely to include the human infrastructure reforms (although the extent of planned retirements has probably gone beyond original PLA expectations), professionalization and regularization of the PLA, and the understanding that spillover effects will allow later acceleration of the pace of military modernization.[16]

A further explanation for the success of the reformist leaders is the nature of the opposition itself. Although such reformist policies as the more radical economic reforms, the restoration of PLA ranks, and the relative deemphasis of Maoist principles, have been opposed by older PLA cadre, their resistance has been unorganized and passive. Both Harlan Jencks and Harvey Nelsen have noted the reluctance most PLA officers have in becoming involved in political issues, preferring instead to concentrate on patently military concerns.[17] This seems to have worked in the Dengists' favor, allowing them the time and opportunity to consolidate political alliances.

Furthermore, the policies that have been introduced to reform personnel and educational policies have long-term implications on the nature of the PLA. A younger, professional, and technically-oriented PLA leadership is likely to have even less of a desire to become actively involved in politics. Harlan Jencks has already documented the apolitical tendencies of younger officers, attributing these feelings to the different experiences of the older cadre who served in an army during the 1930s and 1940s that was highly involved with communist party politics.[18]

However, it should be stressed that a more apolitical PLA leadership is highly contingent upon the assumption that current policies will continue to be pursued under a stable, authoritative regime. In short, Deng Xiaoping's ability to continue his policies is a key variable in assessing the future of the PLA's political role.

Regardless of any apolitical tendencies within the PLA, for a number of reasons it would be inaccurate to ignore it as a major political actor. First, as long as politically active officers such as Ye Jianying and Li Desheng remain in positions of authority, the PLA will continue to wield political clout. Second, the historic Chinese concern of ultimate control over the military will continue to necessitate some sort of co-opting of the PLA leadership through inclusion in policymaking bodies such as the party Central Committee and the Politburo. Therefore, while a reduced PLA role is likely, this is merely a reduction in involvement compared to the 1970s when the military dominated most party policymaking bodies.

The PLA and Chinese Society

An important side effect of the reforms has been the lowering of the PLA's prestige with the peasants. Given the economic opportunities inherent in the "responsibility system," the peasant no longer views service in the PLA as the surest path to success. In fact, many see the PLA as a burden which threatens to enlist family members who then will be lost from productive activity. Other factors causing friction between the army and the populace have been the granting of special privileges to demobilized soldiers and officers, including assignment to coveted positions in the communes or factories, and the retention by PLA units of public buildings and facilities occupied by the military during the Cultural Revolution.

This problem is likely to increase as recruitment policies intended to increase the numbers of urban, technically-proficient soldiers are instituted. These measures, coupled with the planned demobilizations of approximately one million soldiers, will dramatically change the demographic characteristics of the Chinese army, threatening the current portrayal of the PLA as a peasant army which serves as an agent of national integration.

IMPLICATIONS OF THE LINKAGES BETWEEN INTERNATIONAL AND DOMESTIC SYSTEMS

There are three linkages which connect the world system with changes in the Chinese military system. The first, Chinese strategy, links changes in the PLA to the military image Beijing projects internationally. Secondly, China's use of force as a diplomatic signalling mechanism elevates PLA capabilities to a means of communicating Chinese interests to other nations. Last, foreign military purchases are an international transaction which have the capability of changing PLA capabilities.

Capabilities and Strategic Doctrine

Paul Godwin has noted that the Chinese are pursuing a short-term goal of improving the combat effectiveness of their forces. This is being done through selected equipment improvements in PLA units located in key areas. As Wendy Frieman observed, this policy is augumented by importing advanced technology to overcome identified specific problems.

The current educational and personnel reforms are intended to create a military force structure capable of using modern weapons when they are available. In the meantime, the leadership has opted to revise the strategic doctrine of the PLA, labelling this "People's War Under Modern Conditions." As the name implies, there are both continuities and differences from previous Chinese policy. Foremost among the changes are the recognized need to defend key industrial centers and to fight a modern, "combined arms" war.

These changes have resulted from a leadership assessment of the major threats to China's security. While the Soviet Union is believed to pose the most dangerous threat to China, Beijing has decided that this threat is not immediate. Therefore, the Dengists have been able to justify a slowly paced military modernization which emphasizes the capability to deter and, if necessary, defend against Soviet military invasion.

Under the slogan of "People's War under Modern Conditions," Beijing has made acceptable changes to Chinese defense doctrine while maintaining the PLA's image of a strong force which is capable of defending an industralizing China against an army capable of rapid "combined arms" warfare. Concurrently, China maintains the advantages of the original People's War strategy-- the prospect of fighting a protracted war on Chinese soil against the entire Chinese population.

There are two implications of these policies. First, as John Frankenstein has noted, they represent a conscious Chinese leadership decision and therefore reflect their relative comfort with the nation's current ability to deter aggressors. Second, significant changes to Chinese capabilities will take place only over the long-term, and short-term PLA force improvements will only marginally affect China's military power.

Chinese Use of Force

The leadership's continued willingness to use the PLA as a foreign policy instrument in limited operations was demonstrated in the 1979 Sino-Vietnamese War. However, the Chinese experienced far more difficulty in achieving their military objectives than they had anticipated.[19] Additionally, when one considers that the Chinese faced poorly equipped and prepared Vietnamese militia and border units, then it may well be that the Sino-Vietnamese War was a catalyst which prompted the PLA's acceptance of reforms prior to hardware modernization.

Current Chinese military modernization plans indicate that the PLA's combat capability will not change substantially over the near term, and this will definitely affect their use of force during this period. However, over the long-term, assuming successful PLA modernization, it is possible that the Chinese will demonstrate a greater willingness to resort to force. However, this conclusion is highly tentative, since a decision to use force is dependent upon a number of other variables as well.

Foreign Military Purchases

Purchasing foreign military equipment is a means by which the PLA can conceivably increase its combat effectiveness over the near term. However, there are several obstacles to such purchases. Foremost among these is the fact that the PLA's needs far exceed the Chinese ability to pay, while assimilating modern equipment into the defense establishment, reconciling the Chinese xenophobic sense of nationalism with the need for foreign imports, and the West's decision to sell only defensive weapons to China, are additional problems.

The decision not to rely on foreign imports does not mean that Beijing has decided to forego any purchases of foreign military equipment. While foreign currency reserves have been rising due to Chinese arms sales abroad, Beijing has continued to discuss weapon systems purchases with Western nations. The intent of these discussions appears to be twofold--to provide prototypes to develop Chinese versions of the equipment and to provide short-term quick fixes in areas deemed critical by the high command.

In sum, the Western governments and the Chinese have begun to rationalize their policies, thereby making future arms purchases more likely. However, such purchases are likely to provide only marginal improvements in the PLA's capabilities because these sales likely will be of a limited nature and arranged so as to limit Sino-Western interaction. Therefore, foreign imports are likely to have few far-reaching systemic implications for either the Chinese or the West.

SUMMARY

In conclusion, China is pursuing a strategy of reforming the human infrastructure of the PLA while deferring any major hardware modernization efforts. This strategy is based on two related arguments. First, the Chinese military must be staffed, organized, and trained to use modern equipment before such equipment is deployed. Second, the scarcity of resources would make any large scale effort to modernize PLA equipment an unacceptable burden on the Chinese economy.

There remain significant obstacles to this policy of Chinese military modernization, including the old cadres' fear that human infrastructure reforms are proceeding too rapidly, and the lack of horizontal lines of communication which would increase the efficiency of Chinese institutions.

Despite these obstacles the Chinese leadership is pressing on and, although the programs are relatively new, some implications already are apparent. Internationally, the Chinese have demonstrated a willingness to increase participation in arms control discussions and to sell arms without political strings in order to obtain foreign currency to support the modernization efforts. Domestically, the dominance of the professionalization and regularization themes have led to a deemphasis of politics in the PLA, the replacement of older cadres with younger, better educated officers, and an emphasis on learning how to fight a modern war. These trends have two possible implications for the future. First, a younger, technically-oriented PLA leadership could be less inclined to assume a political role than past leaders have. Secondly, a PLA composed of an increasing number of urban educated soldiers is likely to result in a change in the role and status that the PLA historically has enjoyed within Chinese society.

A number of variables will affect the success of the Chinese military modernization program. While a key variable is a stable international environment, the most important factor will continue to be the maintenance of a stable, authoritative regime. This, by implication, means the continued ability of Deng Xiaoping and his followers to dominate Chinese policy.

A number of theoretical implications also have been identified. While international systems theories have flourished, systemic models concerning China, and particularly the PLA, have remained undeveloped. While conflictual models have dominated Chinese military analysis, no comprehensive analytical framework has been proposed to explain events concerning the PLA and its role in China.

While systems theories tend to obscure conflict and conflict has seemed to characterize Chinese policy formulation, if Deng Xiaoping's policies are continued and prove successful, then a greater degree of institutional stability will come to dominate Chinese politics. Given such a trend, some form or hybrid of a systems model can be developed which might begin to provide a more comprehensive explanatory capability concerning the Chinese military. In a curious sense, then, the future of systems theories as applied to China and the future of current Chinese military modernization plans are linked, since both are dependent upon the continued political strength of Deng Xiaoping and his allies.

NOTES

1. The views presented in this paper are those of the author and are not necessarily those of the United States Military Academy, the Department of the Army, or components of the Department of Defense.

2. For discussions of each of these theories, see Robert O. Keohane and Joseph S. Nye, _Power and Interdependence: World Politics in Transition_ (Boston: Little, Brown, and Co., 1977); John Spanier, _Games Nations Play_ (New York: Holt, Reinhart and Winston, 1984); and James E. Doughtery and Robert L. Pfaltzgraff Jr., _Contending Theories of International Relations Theory: A Comprehensive Survey_, 2d ed. (New York: Harper and Reed, 1981).

3. Chinese scholars from the Academy of Social Sciences and the Ministry of Foreign Affairs have studied arms control issues at institutions such as the Rand Corporation, the Hoover Institution, the Fletcher School of Tufts University, Harvard University, Johns Hopkin's School of Advanced International Studies, and Princeton's Woodrow Wilson School.

4. Jonathan D. Pollack, "The Study of Chinese Military Politics: Toward a Framework for Analysis," in Catherine Kelleher (ed.), _Political-Military Systems: Comparative Perspectives_ (Beverley Hills: Sage Publications, 1974), p. 239.

5. See Harlan W. Jencks, From Muskets to Missiles: Politics and Professionalism in the Chinese Army, 1945-1981 (Boulder, CO: Westview Press, 1982); and Harvey W. Nelson, The Chinese Military System: An Organizational Study of the Chinese People's Liberation Army, 2d ed., (Boulder, CO: Westview Press, 1981).

6. The military cleavages have been taken, with modifications, from Jonathan Pollack's article identified above.

7. These models are decidedly not systemic in nature. However, systems models tend to obscure conflict which is an important element in understanding the PLA. The foregoing was the result of a discussion with William Heaton on 12 June 1985.

8. For instance see: Xu Xiangqian, "Heighten Vigilance, Be Ready to Fight," Hongqi (Beijing), July 1978, in Foreign Broadcast Information Service, Daily Report, People's Republic of China (FBIS/PRC), 1 August 1978, pp. E-4 - E-15; Nie Rongzhen, Speech at the August 1978 National Militia Work Conference, Beijing Xinhua Domestic Service, 7 August 1978, in FBIS/PRC, 9 August 1978, p. E-6; and Ye Jianying, Speech at the May-June 1978 Army Political Work Conference, Beijing Xinhua Domestic Service, 5 June 1978, in FBIS/PRC, 5 June 1978, pp. E-12 - E-19.

9. See William W. Whitson, The Chinese High Command: A History of Communist Military Politics, 1927-71 (New York: Praeger Publishers, 1973). For one of the best critiques of the field army model see William L. Parish, Jr., "Factions in Chinese Military Politics," China Quarterly, no. 56 (October/December 1973): 667-699.

10. Nelsen, pp. 148-150.

11. Ibid., pp. 150-152.

12. Ibid., pp. 151-152.

13. Chinese published reports, which generally under-report defense expenditures by as much as 50%, stated that the 1984 national defense expenditures were 12% of the total state budget. See Ronald G. Mitchell, "Chinese Defense Spending in Transition," in Joint Economic Committee, Congress of the United States, China Under the Four Modernizations, Part 1, (Washington, DC: Government Printing Office, 1982), pp. 605-610, for a discussion on the Chinese under-reporting of their defense budget.

14. At the 12th Party Congress in August 1982, 36% of the members of the Politburo and 22% of the members of the Central Committee had extensive PLA experience. Based on data available in Wolfgong Barke and Peter Schier, China's New Party Leadership, Biographies and Analysis of the Twelfth Central Committee of the Chinese Communist Party (Armonk, NY: M.E. Sharpe, Inc., 1985).

15. Such a statement does not mean that the author considers the PLA a united group in the political arena. The term PLA is meant to represent likely consensus views among top PLA leaders.

16. The foregoing was the result of a discussion with William Heaton on 12 June 1985.

17. Jencks, pp. 255-256; Nelsen pp. 27-34; and pp. 126-136.

18. Jencks, pp. 264, 266.

19. See Harlan Jencks, "China's 'Punitive' War on Vietnam: A Military Assessment," *Asian Survey*, vol. 19, no. 8 (August 1978): 801-815.

About the Editors and Contributors

Editors

Lieutenant Colonel CHARLES D. LOVEJOY, JR., U.S. Army, is currently the Professor of Military Science at Princeton University. Prior to this assignment, he served on the faculty of the Defense Intelligence College, Washington, D.C. As an Army China area specialist, he has taught at West Point and served as the Politico-Military Officer for China on the Army Staff. He is currently completing a comprehensive analysis of contemporary Catholic Church relations with China.

Commander BRUCE W. WATSON, U.S. Navy, is the Director of Publications at the Defense Intelligence College and is an Adjunct Professor in the School of Foreign Service, Georgetown University. Dr. Watson is the author of Red Navy at Sea: Soviet Naval Operations on the High Seas, 1956-1980. He has also coedited several books including The Military Lessons of the Falkland Islands War, Military Intelligence and Universities, American Intervention in Grenada, The Soviet Navy: Strengths and Liabilities, and The Soviet Navy As We Approach the Twenty-First Century. Dr. Watson is coauthoring a study on Soviet, Cuban, and U.S. interests in the Caribbean, and currently serves as the Chairman, Comparative Foreign Policy Section, International Studies Association.

Contributors

JOHN FRANKENSTEIN is Associate Professor of International Studies at the American Graduate School of International Management ("Thunderbird"), Glendale, Arizona, where he teaches courses on modern China, international relations, international defense industries, and political risk assessment. Before opting for the academic life, Dr. Frankenstein was a Chinese language officer in the U.S. Foreign Service; he also served in the U.S. Navy in Southeast Asia. He has published on China in Problems of Communism, Asian Wall Street Journal, Management Review and elsewhere. In 1984 he was the Thunderbird Exchange Professor at Beijing's University of International Business and Economics.

WENDY FRIEMAN has recently been appointed Senior Research Scientist in Science Applications International Corporation's Asia Technology Program. She performs research on Chinese military modernization, Chinese science and technology; technology transfer to Asia; Japanese international trade and R&D management policies; and U.S.-China trade and security relations. Previously, Ms. Frieman was a China consultant with the Research and Analysis Division of SRI International. She received her Bachelor's and Master's degrees from Stanford University and has published numerous articles and reports on Chinese and Japanese industry and foreign trade.

PAUL H. B. GODWIN is professor of national security policy at the National War College. He is a coauthor of The Making of a Model Citizen in Communist China; editor and contributor to The Chinese Defense Establishment: Continuity and Change in the 1980's; a contributor to Civil-Military Relations in Communist Societies, edited by Dale Herspring and Ivan Volgyes; China and the World: Foreign Policy in the Post-Mao Era, edited by Samuel S. Kim; Chinese Defense Policy, edited by Gerald Segal and William T. Tow; and Modernizing CHina: Post-Mao Reform and Modernization, edited by A. Doak Barnett and Ralph Clough. Dr. Godwin has also published articles in numerous journals, including Comparative Politics, Studies in Comparative Communism, Contemporary China, and Small Group Behavior.

WILLIAM R. HEATON, JR., is an estimates officer with the National Intelligence Council. Prior to that he served as a member of the faculty of the National War College and the U.S. Air Force Academy. He is the coauthor of two books, and the author of numerous articles on Asian political affairs.

Captain ROBERT E. JOHNSON, JR., U.S. Army, is an Assistant Professor teaching comparative and Chinese politics at the United States Military Academy. He received a Masters of Arts in Law and Diplomacy from The Fletcher School, where he is currently a doctoral candidate writing his dissertation on recent Chinese military reforms. He was a research fellow at the Defense Intelligence College and the Sandhurst Soviet Studies Centre in England during 1985 where he conducted research on the Chinese military system. He is also coauthor of an article on Northeast Asian security issues in Daniel J. Kaufman and Michael L. Brown's International Security Issues: A Regional Approach (forthcoming).

Lieutenant Colonel RICHARD J. LATHAM, U.S. Air Force, is the Air Attache (Liaison Officer) to Hong Kong. He previously served as the Special Assistant to the Director of Estimates for China Affairs, Headquarters U.S. Air Force, and as Director of Comparative and Area Studies, Department of Political Science, U.S. Air Force Academy. He holds a Ph.D. in politics from the University of Washington and has published several articles on Chinese defense policy and post-Mao reforms.

ROBERT G. SUTTER is the Head of the Asia-Latin America Section at the Congressional Research Service and teaches at Georgetown University and the University of Virginia. A frequent visitor to China, Dr. Sutter is the author of several books and articles including *China Watch: Toward Sino-American Reconciliation*, *Chinese Foreign Policy After the Cultural Revolution*, *China Quandry: Domestic Determinants of U.S. China Policy, 1972-1982*, and *Chinese Foreign Policy: Developments After Mao*.

WILLIAM T. TOW is Assistant Professor of International Relations, University of Southern California. He has co-edited books on East Asian security affairs, including works on Chinese defense issues, Japanese and ANZUS security problems as well as on U.S. foreign and strategic approaches toward the Asian Pacific. He has also authored many journal articles, including pieces in *Asian Survey*, *International Affairs*, *Pacific Affairs*, *Problems of Communism* and *Survival*. Dr. Tow is currently working on a project dealing with overall Western alliance politics and on a book assessing the U.S.-PRC-Japanese geopolitical relationship.

Index

Academy of Electronic Technology, 45
Academy of Military Science, 22, 95
Academy of Sciences, 66, 73
"Active defense," 3, 22, 23
ADMs. *See* Atomic demolition munitions
Advanced Infantry School (Shijiazhuang), 93, 96
Aeronautics Industry, Ministry of, 59
Affordable force structure (AFS), 40(fig.), 41, 42, 43
AFS. *See* Affordable force structure
Agriculture, 17, 37, 38
Air-to-air missile
  Atoll, 53(table), 57
Aircraft, combat, 2, 53(table), 56, 57, 63, 64, 76-77, 78, 82, 85, 101
  fixed-wing, 1, 8
  H-5s, 76
  H-6s, 76
  J-4s, 57
  J-6s, 53(table), 56, 57, 58, 76
  J-8, 76
  MiG-21s, 76, 85
  number of, 71, 76
  optical system. *See* Float glass technology
  Q-5, 53(table), 56, 58, 76
  TU-16, 103
  See also Helicopters; Navy, air power
Air force, 6, 8-9, 15, 28, 58, 71, 95, 103, 120

construction, 16
manpower, 71, 81, 87, 93
naval, 8
See also Aircraft, combat
Airmobile forces, 7
Alexander, A. J., 73, 74
Amnesty International, 37
Antiaircraft guns, 57, 58
Anti-armor technology, 62, 71
Antitank munitions, 7, 53(table), 78
ANZUS. *See* Australia, New Zealand, United States Pact
Armored personnel carriers, 1, 53(table), 57
Armor School, 96
Arms
  captured, 60
  coproduction, 51, 53(table), 55-56, 59-60, 62, 65
  modifications, 53(table), 58, 61, 75-77
  sales, 51, 76, 77-78, 79, 114, 115, 123-124
  transfers, 45, 52, 62, 78, 114, 120
  See also Conventional weapons; Defense industrial base; Nuclear arms control; Nuclear weapons; Reverse engineering
Arms race, 108
Artillery, 1, 57, 63, 82
ASEAN. *See* Association of South East Asian Nations
Asian balance of power, 101
Association of South East Asian Nations (ASEAN), 28, 113
ATM (antitank missile). *See* Antitank munitions

133

Atomic demolition munitions (ADMs), 105
Australia, 53(table)
Australia, New Zealand, United States (ANZUS) Pact, 87
Automation, 61, 82
Automotive Industry Corporation, 65
Automotive technology, 65
Avionics, 9, 78

"Back-door clique behavior," 17
Balance of power. See Asian balance of power; Power politics
Baotou (Inner Mongolia), 102
Beijing Institute for Strategic Studies (BISS), 6
Beijing military region, 4, 118
Beijing Radio, 94
Beijing Review, 86
BISS. See Beijing Institute for Strategic Studies
Bok, Georges Tan Eng, 3
Bombers. See Aircraft, combat, TU-16
Border defense, 4, 5, 8, 70, 71, 101
Border wars, 11
Bureaucracy, 18, 73
 reform, 36, 37
 See also Internecine bureaucratic strife

CAD/CAM. See Technology, computer-aided design/computer-aided manufacturing
Carter, Jimmy, 51
Casting technology, 63
CCP. See Chinese Communist Part
CDSTI. See Commission of Defense Science, Technology and Industry
Centralized planning, 38, 39, 41, 42
Chiang Kai-shek, 86
China Daily (Beijing), 78, 82
China International Trust and Investment Corporation, 73
Chinese Communist Party (CCP), 86, 116
 "cadre-scientists," 18
 Central Committee, 92, 121
 Eleventh Party Congress, Third Plenum (1978), 36, 41, 80
 Military Commission, 92, 93, 95
 military line, 3. See also People's Liberation Army, and CCP
 Politburo, 121
 reforms, 36. See also Post-Mao reforms
 Twelfth Party Congress, 20
 See also Ideological factionalization; Political leadership; *Red Flag*
Chinese Military History Museum (Beijing), 78
Chinese Working Group, 27
City defense, 5. See also Underground facilities
Civil Air Defense, 8
Civil defense program. See Civil Air Defense
Civil-military relations. See Defense industrial base, and civilian industries; People's Liberation Army, and CCP
COCOM. See Coordinating Committee of the Consultative Group
Combined arms tactics, 7, 8, 9, 81, 85, 87, 122, 123
Command, control, communications and intelligence (C^3I), 16, 22, 23
Command and control systems, 91, 105, 106
Commission of Defense Science, Technology and Industry (CDSTI), 73, 78, 82, 84
Computers, 27, 61, 64, 82, 105
Consumerism, 38, 39, 42, 43, 44, 45
Conventional forces, 16, 25, 87
Conventional weapons, 1, 4, 22, 23, 25, 60. See also Soviet-designed conventional arms
Coordinating Committee (COCOM) of the Consultative Group, 27, 115, 116
CSS-NX-3. See Submarine-launched ballistic missile
CSS-2 (IRBM), 25, 53(table)
C^3I. See Command, control, communications and intelligence

Cultural Revolution. *See under* Mao Zedong

"Daring to become rich," 37, 38
Decentralized planning, 38, 67
Defendory International Exhibit (1984), 45
Defense industrial base, 1, 6, 15, 17, 29-30(n2), 65-67, 82-85, 122
  budget, 41, 42, 45
  and civilian industries, 16, 20, 44, 45, 66-67, 73, 84
  and foreign technology, 52, 60-62, 63, 67, 73, 83. *See also* Arms; Technology
  investment, 41, 42, 43, 45
  manpower, 74
  organization, 73
  production, 53(table), 54-55, 56, 58, 60, 61, 63, 84. *See also* Arms, coproduction
  production capacity, 40(fig.), 43
  retooling, 44
  segregated, 42-43
  urban, 5, 70
Defense infrastructure, 15, 20, 64
Defense Intelligence Agency (DIA) (U.S.), 87
Democracy Wall, 37
Democratic procedures, 36, 37
Deng Xiaoping, 18, 19, 21, 26, 28, 70, 80, 81, 91, 111
  and PLA, 92, 94, 98, 112, 113, 118, 121, 125
Destroyers, 53(table)
  Luda-class, 120
Deterrence. *See* Strategic nuclear deterrence; War deterrence
DIA. *See* Defense Intelligence Agency
Domestic reforms. *See* Post-Mao reforms

Early warning radar, 53(table), 105
Economic efficiency, 38, 42, 43
Economic Management (journal), 84
Economic planning, 26. *See also* Centralized planning

Economic reform, 36, 37, 38, 43-45, 59, 65, 73, 81
Egalitarianism, 37, 38
Egypt, 76
Electronic countermeasures, 57, 64
Electronics, 16, 22, 23, 54, 57, 61, 63, 64, 65, 78
Electronics Industry, Ministry of, 65
"Electronic vs. steel" debate (1970s), 120
Energy shortfalls, 42
Engine construction, 16, 59, 61, 77
Engineers, 74, 75, 85. *See also* Science and technology, personnel
European peace movement, 108

Falklands war, 93
Fire control and self-propulsion systems, 78, 82
Fire control radar, 78
"Five principles of peaceful coexistence," 116
Five-year plan, sixth, 65
Float glass technology, 53(table), 63
Foreign affairs reforms, 36
Foreign exchange, 77, 115, 124
Forward defense, 6
Four Modernizations (1978-1988), 17, 18, 19, 25, 38
  priorities, 112, 119
France, 26
  and China, 59-62
  Mirage aircraft, 120
Frankenstein, John, 115, 116, 123
Frieman, Wendy, 115, 122
Fuzhou military industries, 73

Gang of four, 117
Gaseous diffusion separation plant (Lanzhou), 102
General Logistics Department, 10
Geng Biao, 19
Geographic scope, 24
Geopolitical factors, 25, 28-29
Germany, 53(table)
Godwin, Paul H. B., 22, 81, 115, 117, 118, 122
Gold, 77

"Golden rice bowl," 41
GPD. *See* People's Liberation Army, General Political Department
Great Britain
 and China, 53(table), 59, 63, 76
 F-4 Phantoms, 76
 Harrier aircraft, 120
Ground warfare, 9, 28
Guidance and control systems, 64
Gyrocompasses, 64

Handbook of the Chinese People's Liberation Army (DIA), 87
Han Huaizhi, 93
Hawk surface-to-air missile (U.S.), 9
Heator, William R. J., 112, 115, 117
Helicopters, 7, 53(table), 62
 Bell, 77
 Dauphin-2, 59
Heymann, Hans, 57, 74
High-tech industries, 52, 84
Hong Kong, 27
Hongqi. See Red Flag
HOT (weapon system), 78
Household production responsibility, 37
Hua Guofeng, 93
Hu Yaobang, 87

IAEA. *See* International Atomic Energy Agency
ICBMs. *See* Intercontinental ballistic missiles
Ideological factionalization, 15, 16, 18, 30(n6)
IISS. *See* International Institute for Strategic Studies
India, 11, 101
Industry, 17, 21, 25, 42, 70
 basic, 55
 reforms, 38, 65
 See also Defense industrial base
Infantry Command School, 97
Infrared equipment, 63, 64, 75
Inner Mongolia, 102
Innovation, 69, 74, 85
Instrumentation, 61, 64, 82, 105

Integrated circuit and computer production, 16
Intercontinental ballistic missiles (ICBMs), 1, 10, 53(table), 54, 82, 101, 103-104, 106
Interdependence, 114-115, 116
Intermediate-range ballistic missiles (IRBMs), 25, 53(table), 54, 101, 103
International Atomic Energy Agency (IAEA), 107
International Institute for Strategic Studies (IISS), 71, 87, 88, 103
International peace movement, 114
International system, 112-116, 122-124, 125. *See also* National security policy, international influences
Internecine bureaucratic strife, 15, 16
Iran, 114
Iraq, 76, 114
IRBMs. *See* Intermediate-range ballistic missiles
"Iron rice bowl," 37, 97

Jane's, 52, 75
Japan, 26, 27, 28, 70, 114
 and China, 53(table), 63
Jeeps, 77
Jencks, Harlan W., 116, 121
Jiefangjun Bao. See Liberation Army Daily
Jiefangjun Huabao. See Liberation Army Pictorial
Jingji Guanli. See Economic Management
J-35B *Draken* (Swedish aircraft), 76

Keyworth, George, 29
Khrushchev, Nikita, 54
KMT. *See* Kuomintang period
Korea, 70, 101
Korean war, 11
Kuomintang (KMT) period, 82, 83

Landsat ground station, 64
Lanzhou, 102
Lanzhou military region, 4
Lasers, 63, 64, 75, 82

Latham, Richard J., 70, 114, 115, 116
"Left ideology," 92, 95-96, 98, 117
Lenin, V. I., 96
Liaowang (weekly), 92
Liberalization, 37, 59
Liberation Army Daily, 19
Liberation Army Pictorial, 78
Licensing, 76, 77
Li Desheng, 121
Lin Biao, 19, 21, 93, 102
Liu Huaqing, 118
Logistical support system, 4, 5, 6
"Long Marchers," 19
Lovejoy, Charles D., Jr., 111

Machine Building Industries, 20
Machine guns, 53(table), 57
Machine tools, 83-84
Manchuria, 4, 22, 70
Maoist doctrine, 19, 25, 117-118, 121
Mao Zedong, 18, 54, 96
  agricultural policy, 37
  and Cultural Revolution, 86, 93, 117
  death (1976), 102
  military thought, 3, 5, 6, 10, 11, 22, 24, 42, 80
Mao Zedong's Military Writings, 93
Market economies, 17, 38-39
Marxism, 28
Marxism-Leninism, 11, 18
Medium-range ballistic missile (MRBM), 53(table), 101, 103
Microwave technology, 64
Milan missile, 78
Military academies, 80, 92-94, 96, 97, 98
Military art, 3
Military Balance (IISS), 71, 87
Military-civilian production boards, 20
Military doctrine, 1, 2, 3-4, 10, 16, 22, 81, 85, 91, 95, 115, 123
  defined, 2-3
Military hierarchy, 2, 9, 16, 17, 22, 91, 112, 117-118, 119, 124

Military operations, 1, 3, 4, 5, 6, 7-8, 10-11
Military regions, 4, 71
Military science, 3
Military Service Law, 85, 117
Military strategy, 1, 2, 3, 4-8, 9-10, 11, 15, 22-25, 35, 36, 94, 95, 122
  levels, 3
  See also National security policy
Military tactics, 3, 22, 94
Militia, 117
MIRVed. *See* Multiple, independently targeted strategic nuclear delivery vehicles
MND. *See* National Defense, Ministry of
Mobile warfare, 6, 7, 28
Mongolian People's Republic, 4
"Mountaintopism," 17, 118-119
MRBM. *See* Medium-range ballistic missile
MRVs. *See* Multiple reentry vehicles
Multiple, independently targeted (MIRVed) strategic nuclear delivery vehicles, 24
Multiple reentry vehicles (MRVs), 105
Multiple rocket launcher, 53(table)
Munitions Control List (U.S.), 27

National Defense, Ministry of (MND), 44, 66, 73
National Defense Industries Offices, 44
National security policy, 2, 69
  domestic influences, 35, 36, 39, 40, 41-45, 69, 70, 86, 111, 117-123, 124
  international influences, 35, 39-41, 69, 70-72, 85, 86, 102, 106, 107, 108, 112, 124.
  See also International system
  risk, 41
NATO. *See* North Atlantic Treaty Organization
Navy, 15, 95, 120
  air power, 8
  commander of, 118
  manpower, 71, 87, 93

surface combatants, 71
  See also People's Liberation Army, Naval Academy
NDSTIC. *See* State Commission of Science, Technology, and Industry for National Defense
Nelson, Harvey W., 116, 118, 121
New Zealand, 87
Nien rebellion, 86
Nie Rongzhen, 66, 117
Ningxia province, 7, 105
Non-aligned power, 28, 113
North Atlantic Treaty Organization (NATO), 22
North central China, 4, 105
North China Industries Corporation, 73
Northeast China, 6, 70, 71
Nuclear arms control, 106-108, 114, 116, 124
Nuclear-powered ballistic missile submarine (SSBN), 1, 23, 54
Nuclear weapons, 1, 2, 4, 15, 24, 25, 54-55, 61, 66, 85, 101-106, 107, 120
  battlefield, 7, 105
  deployment, 104
  fission test, first (1964), 54, 102
  fusion. *See* Thermonuclear weapon
  strike capabilities, 103, 104, 107
  testing, 102, 104
  See also Nuclear arms control; Strategic nuclear deterrence

Offensive operations, 6
Offshore oil exploration, 64, 87
Ordnance Ministry, 73
"Over the horizon" capabilities, 4

Pakistan, 102
Paratroops, 7
Patent law, 79
Patrol craft, 53(table)
Peace movement, 108, 114
Peasant conscript, 21, 96, 122
People's Air Defense. *See* Civil Air Defense
People's Daily, 19, 80, 82, 84
People's Armed Police, 88
People's Liberation Army (PLA)
  armored divisions, 71, 75-76, 82, 87
  artillery division, 87
  border troop division, 71
  budget, 20, 21, 121
  and CCP, 16, 19-20, 26-27, 29, 65, 80-81, 91, 92, 93, 117, 119, 121, 124
  and Chinese society, 122, 124
  conflict within, 117-120
  education programs, 63-64, 80, 81, 92-98, 115, 117
  exercises, 7, 8, 105
  force deployment, 71
  force structure, 1, 10, 72, 80, 87. *See also* National security policy
  General Political Department (GPD), 19, 20, 23
  General Staff, 118
  General Staff, Training Department, 94-95
  as "Great Wall of Steel," 82
  ground divisions, 15, 71, 76, 87, 120
  institutional structure, 119-120
  and interpersonal relations, 118-119, 120
  interservice rivalry, 120
  local force divisions, 71, 87, 88
  main force units, 87-88
  manpower, 15, 21, 71, 72(fig.), 87-88, 96, 117, 122, 124
  Military Academy, 92, 93, 95, 96
  modernization, 1, 2, 3, 10, 15, 16, 24, 51, 62-67, 80-85, 86, 91, 94, 111, 112, 124-125. *See also* International system; Military doctrine; Military operations; Military strategy; National security policy; Science and technology
  modernization costs, 22
  Naval Academy, 93
  officer corps, 1, 10, 19, 81, 93, 94, 95, 96-97, 98, 121,

124
and political education, 94, 117
press organs, 20
professionalism, 1, 91, 96, 97, 98, 117-118, 121
promotion system. See "Mountaintopism"
and ranks, 117, 121
regional deployment, 23
retirement, 121
in Vietnam, 5, 11, 57, 65, 95, 123
weapons, 1, 2, 3, 4, 6, 7, 10, 15, 17, 21, 22, 23, 24, 27, 51, 52-67, 72, 80, 82, 86, 124. See also Arms; Conventional weapons; Nuclear weapons; Technology; *individual types*
see also Air Force; Beijing Institute for Strategic Studies; Defense industrial base; Navy; Second Artillery
People's War, 5, 7, 9, 10, 22, 23, 25, 36, 42, 65, 91, 117, 123
"People's War Under Modern Conditions," 1, 3, 10, 22, 24, 36, 80, 81, 120, 122, 123
PFS. See Producible force structure
Pilkington Brothers (British company), 63
PLA. See People's Liberation Army
Plant imports, 77
Pluralism, 37
Plutonium production reactors (Baotou), 102
Political culture, 86
Political leadership, 15, 16-19, 82, 111-112, 123, 125
purges (1971), 102
See also People's Liberation Army, and CCP; Pragmatists
Political reform, 81, 86
Political strategy, 2, 5
Pollack, Jonathan D., 116
Polytechnic (Chinese corporation), 73, 78
Positional defense, 6, 22
Post-Mao reforms, 36-45, 91, 111, 112
Power politics, 113-114, 115, 116
Pragmatists, 26, 29
Pratt & Whitney aircraft engines, 53(table)
Pre-emption, 25
Price system, 26, 44
Producible force structure (PFS), 40(fig.), 41, 42, 44
Professional elites. See Technocrats
Profitability emphasis, 38, 42, 43, 44, 73, 84
Protraction, 6, 24, 25

Qian Xuesen, 66
Qing dynasty, 82, 83, 86
Qin Jinwei, 118
Quality control, 84

Radar, 53(table), 62, 64, 78, 105
R&D. See Research and development
RDT&E. See Research, development, testing and evaluation
Reactors, 102
Red Army of Workers and Peasants, 10
Red Flag, 20, 66, 78, 80
Red Guard movement (1960s), 102
Renmin Ribao. See People's Daily
Research, development, testing and evaluation (RDT&E), 1
Research and development (R&D), 41, 42, 45, 53(table), 54, 55-56, 61, 65, 74, 112
budget, 18, 102
investment, 42
Reserve forces, 6
Resource management, 18, 84
Reverse engineering, 53(table), 56-58, 60, 61, 77
Robinson, Thomas W., 25
Rolls Royce (British company), 59, 63, 65, 76
Romance of the Three Kingdoms, The, 116

Sagger missile, 78
SALT. See Strategic Arms Limitation Talks
SAM. See Surface-to-air missile units
Satellites, 54, 61, 64

intelligence, 105
reconnaissance, 2, 105
research, 105
SA-2 missile systems (Soviet), 8
Science and technology (S&T), 15, 16-19, 38, 65, 66, 80, 83
  infrastructure, 60
  personnel, 63-64, 66, 74, 80, 112
  training, 94
Scientists, 74-75, 102. *See also* Science and technology, personnel
Second Artillery, 23, 54, 71
Second Field Army, 118
Second-sourcing, 84
Second strike capability, 10, 25
Seismic equipment, 64
Selected Works (Deng), 94
Self-Strengtheners, 78, 82
Sensing technology, 64
Shanghai Communique (1972), 21
Shenyang industrial center (Manchuria), 70
Shenyang military region, 4
Shijie Jingji Daobao. See World Economic Herald
Shipbuilding, 65
Sikorsky Blackhawks, 77
Simon, Dennis Fred, 26, 75
Sino-American Military Technical Cooperation Negotiations, 27
Sino-Soviet dispute (1960), 2, 26
Sino-Western collective defense ties, 28, 29
SLBM. *See* Submarine-launched ballistic missile
"Socialist material civilization," 38
"Socialist spiritual civilization," 38
Sovereignty, 16, 19-21, 27
Soviet-designed conventional arms, 1, 53(table), 75, 76, 85
Soviet Union
  and China, military and technical assistance to, 1-2, 8, 17, 18, 25-26, 53(table), 54, 55-56, 59, 72-73, 75, 101, 102, 104, 115, 123
  and China, war threat, 3, 4, 5-6, 7-8, 9, 11, 21-22, 25, 28, 70-72, 95, 101, 106, 107, 113
  and Europe, 86
  force deployment, 70-71
  MiG-19, 56, 76
  Military-Industrial Commission (VPK), 74
  military technology, 4, 22, 57
  nuclear weapons, 101, 106, 108
  security concerns, 70
  State Committee for Science and Technology, 74
  and United States, 25, 28, 70, 106, 107-108
  and Vietnam, 70
  weapons, 9, 73-74
Space program, 2. *See also* Satellites
Spey aircraft engines, 53(table), 59, 61, 63, 76-77
SSBN. *See* Nuclear-powered ballistic missile submarine
SSTC. *See* State Science and Technology Commission
S&T. *See* Science and Technology
Stalin, Joseph, 25
State Commission of Science, Technology, and Industry for National Defense (NDSTIC), 20, 21
State Council, 73
State Science and Technology Commission (SSTC), 73
State Shipbuilding Corporation, 65
Strategic areas, 22
Strategic Arms Limitation Talks (SALT), 107
Strategic forces, 16, 24, 25
Strategic missile wing, 23
Strategic nuclear deterrence, 7, 10, 22, 23, 24, 28, 36, 107
Strategic rocket forces. *See* Second Artillery
"Streamline the Army to Raise Its Combat Effectiveness" (Deng), 94
Submarine-launched ballistic missile (SLBM), 53(table), 54, 101, 102-103, 104-105, 106

Submarines, 1, 23, 57, 61, 64, 102-103
  Golf-class, 104
  Han-class, 53(table), 54
  nuclear, 82
  number of, 71
  Xia-class, 53(table), 54
Superpowers' hegemonism, 2, 70
Surface acoustic wave devices, 64
Surface-to-air missile (SAM) units, 8, 9
  Guideline, 53(table), 56-57
Sutter, Robert G., 113, 114, 116
Sweden, 76
Systems Engineering--Theory and Practice (journal), 66

Taiping rebellion, 86
Taiwan, 17, 21, 28, 101, 113
Taking war to the enemy as soon as possible, 10-11
Tanks, 1, 2, 7, 53(table), 71, 75-76, 78
  number of, 76
  T-59, 63, 75
  T-62, 75
  T-63, 75
  T-69, 63, 75
Technocrats, 16, 18, 43, 117
"Technological transformation," 83
Technology, 2, 3, 4, 6, 7, 8, 9, 10, 53(table), 78, 82, 86, 114
  computer-aided design/computer-aided manufacturing (CAD/CAM), 61
  exchange, 78
  imported, 16, 20-21, 25, 26, 27, 43, 51, 65, 78, 122. *See also* Defense industrial base, and foreign technology
  and self-reliance, 26, 29, 66, 78-79, 85, 86
  transfer, 27-28, 29, 55, 61, 62-63, 69, 83, 85, 115.
  See also Arms
  See also Science and technology
Thermonuclear weapon (1967), 54, 102, 103
Third World, 17, 21, 28, 44, 45, 114
Threat perceptions. *See* National security policy, international influences; Soviet Union, and China, war threat
Total war, 23
TOW. *See* Tube-launched, optically tracked, wire-guided weapon
Tow, William T., 113, 114, 115, 116, 117, 119
Transportation, 4, 42
Tube-launched, optically tracked, wire-guided (TOW) weapon, 78

Ultra-individualism, 38
Underground facilities, 8
Unified battlefield approach, 22
United Nations disarmament conference (1982), 108
United Nations General Assembly arms control proposals (1983), 108
United States
  and China, 17, 21, 28, 29, 51, 57, 102, 107, 113, 114, 116
  and China, military and technical assistance to, 9, 17, 18, 27, 28-29, 51, 53(table), 62, 63, 64, 67, 77-78
  military technology, 57
  nuclear weapons, 101, 106
  "Sidewinder" missile, 57
  and Taiwan, 17, 28
  See also under Soviet Union
Uranium enrichment, 102
U.S.-Chinese Science and Technology Agreements (1979, 1984), 28
Ussuri Rivier incident (1969), 11

Vertical cliques, 119
Vietnam. *See under* People's Liberation Army; Soviet Union
Volunteerism, 18
"Voornzhenien," 22
VPK. *See* Soviet Union, Military-Industrial Commission

War deterrence, 2, 8, 18, 42, 54, 71
Warfighting, 24, 42
Warsaw Pact, 25

Weapons. *See* Arms; Conventional weapons; Nuclear weapons; Technology; *under* People's Liberation Army
Wei Guoqing, 20
Western Europe, 114
West European defense firms, 27, 62, 63, 78
Whitson, William W., 118
World Economic Herald (Shanghai), 18

Xenophobia, 15, 26, 123
Xian, 59
Xiao Ke, 92, 94, 95, 96, 98
Xia Wenxiang, 45, 114

Xinhua (Chinese News Agency), 92
Xinjiang, 4, 8, 22
Xu Xiangqian, 17, 24, 117

Yang Dezhi, 118
Yang Shangkun, 3, 80-81, 94
Ye Jianying, 117, 121
Yu Qiuli, 20, 23, 81, 94, 96

Zhang Aiping, 5, 19, 20-21, 66, 78, 84-85
Zhang Jingyi, 35, 39
Zhang Tingfa, 74
Zhang Zhen, 81
Zhao Ziyang, 108
Zong He, 6